Psychology of Emotions, Motivations and Actions

SMOKING AS A RISK FACTOR FOR SUICIDE

Psychology of Emotions, Motivations and Actions

Psychology of Aggression
James P. Morgan (Editor)
2004. 1-59454-136-1

New Research on the Psychology of Fear
Paul L. Gower (Editor)
2005. 1-59454-334-8

Impulsivity: Causes, Control and Disorders
George H. Lassiter (Editor)
2009. 978-1-60741-951-8

Handbook of Stress: Causes, Effects and Control
Pascal Heidenreich and Isidor Prüter (Editors)
2009. 978-1-60741-858-0

Handbook of Aggressive Behavior Research
Caitriona Quin and Scott Tawse (Editors)
2009. 978-1-60741-583-1

Handbook of Aggressive Behavior Research
Caitriona Quin and Scott Tawse (Editors)
2009. 978-1-61668-572-0

The Psychology of Pessimism
Daniel X. Choi, Ravi B. DeSilva and John R. T. Monson (Authors)
2010. 978-1-60876-802-8

Psychological Well-Being
Ingrid E. Wells (Editor)
2010. 978-1-61668-180-7

Psychology of Denial
Sofía K. Ogden and Ashley D. Biebers (Editors)
2010. 978-1-61668-094-7

Psychology of Neuroticism and Shame
Raymond G. Jackson (Editor)
2010. 978-1-60876-870-7

Psychology of Hate
Carol T. Lockhardt (Editor)
2010. 978-1-61668-050-3

Bio-Psycho-Social Perspectives on Interpersonal Violence
Martha Frias-Armenta and Victor Corral-Verdigp (Editors)
2010. 978-1-61668-159-3

Psychology of Risk Perception
Joana G. Lavino and Rasmus B. Neumann (Editors)
2010. 978-1-60876-960-5

Psychology of Persuasion
Janos Csapó and Andor Magyar (Editor)
2010. 978-1-60876-590-4

Psychology of Happiness
Anna Mäkinen and Paul Hájek (Editor)
2010. 978-1-60876-555-3

Personal Strivings as a Predictor of Emotional Intelligence
Ferenc Margitics and Zsuzsa Pauwlik (Authors)
2010. 978-1-60876-620-8

Psychology of Thinking
David A. Contreras (Editor)
2010. 978-1-61668-934-6

Psychology of Expectations
Editors: Pablo León and Nino Tamez (Editors)
2010. 978-1-60876-832-5

Cognitive and Neuroscientific Aspects of Human Love: A Guide for Marriage and Couples Counseling
Wiiliam A. Lambos and William C. Emener (Authors)
2010. 978-1-61668-281-1

Psychology of Intuition
Bartoli Ruelas and Vanessa Briseño (Editor)
2010. 978-1-60876-899-8

Extraverted and Energized: Review and Tests of Stress Moderation and Mediation
Dave Korotkov (Author)
2010. 978-1-61668-325-2

Emotion's Effects on Attention and Memory: Relevance to Posttraumatic Stress Disorder
Katherine Mickley Steinmetz and Elizabeth Kensinger (Authors)
2010. 978-1-61668-239-2

Friendships: Types, Cultural, Psychological and Social Aspects
Joan C. Toller (Editor)
2010. 978-1-61668-008-4

Reputation and the Evolution of Generous Behavior
Pat Barclay (Author)
2010. 978-1-61668-402-0

Friendships: Types, Cultural, Psychological and Social Aspects
Joan C. Toller (Editor)
2010. 978-1-61668-386-3

Reputation and the Evolution of Generous Behavior
Pat Barclay (Authors)
2010. 978-1-61668-402-0

Emotion's Effects on Attention and Memory: Relevance to Posttraumatic Stress Disorder
Katherine Mickley Steinmetz and Elizabeth Kensinger (Authors)
2010. 978-1-61668-532-4

Smoking as a Risk Factor for Suicide
Maurizio Pompili (Authors)
2010. 978-1-61668-507-2

Creativity: Fostering, Measuring and Contexts
Alessandra M. Corrigan (Editor)
2010. 978-1-61668-807-3

Personality Traits: Classifications, Effects and Changes
John Paul Villanueva (Editor)
2010. 978-1-61668-619-2

Extraverted and Energized: Review and Tests of Stress Moderation and Mediation
Dave Korotkov (Authors)
2010. 978-1-61668-703-8

Psychological Well-Being
Ingrid E. Wells (Editor)
2010. 978-1-61668-804-2

Smoking as a Risk Factor for Suicide
Maurizio Pompili (Authors)
2010. 978-1-61668-817-2

Psychology of Emotions, Motivations and Actions

SMOKING AS A RISK FACTOR FOR SUICIDE

MAURIZIO POMPILI

Nova Science Publishers, Inc.
New York

For permission to use material from this book please contact us:
Telephone 631-231-7269; Fax 631-231-8175
Web Site: http://www.novapublishers.com

LIBRARY OF CONGRESS CATALOGING-IN-PUBLICATION DATA

Available upon Request
ISBN: 978-1-61668-507-2

Published by Nova Science Publishers, Inc. † New York

CONTENTS

Preface

Cigarette smoking is associated with an increased risk for suicide. However, findings regarding this relationship are not yet consistent. Despite the fact that the prevalence of smoking is higher in suicidal individuals, it is not clear that smoking itself (or the effect of nicotine on brain function) is directly involved in suicidality or whether other factors associated with both suicide and smoking are implicated in this relationship. Indeed it has been found that several suicide risk factors are more common among current smokers than among those who have never smoked. This new book examines the findings in regards to the increased risk in suicide among cigarette smokers.

Chapter 1

THE WORLD HEALTH ORGANIZATION AND TOBACCO

Tobacco use is one of the biggest public health threats the world has ever faced. The WHO (World Health Organization) estimates that there are more than one billion adult smokers in the world, a figure expected to rise to 1.7 billion between 2020-2025. Almost half of the world's children breathe air polluted by tobacco smoke (Guindon & Boisclair, 2003; World Health Organization, 2001, 2009). Tobacco use kills 5.4 million people a year - an average of one person every six seconds - and accounts for one in 10 adult deaths worldwide. Lastly, it is a risk factor for six of the eight leading causes of deaths in the world (see Figure 1).

In the 1950s and 1960s, knowledge of the health consequences of smoking by the general public was minimal, and the first major intervention against tobacco use in the US and in other developed countries was an information shock (Novotny & Mamudu, 2008). In 1964 the Surgeon General published a report on the Health Consequences of Smoking stating that, "Cigarette smoking is a health hazard of sufficient importance in the United States to warrant appropriate remedial action" (U.S. Department of Health EaW, 1964). However, through the late 1980s, the public health response to tobacco use was mostly a set of unsuccessful efforts to gain political footing against the tobacco industry; and only since mid-1980s was smoking recognized as a form of drug addiction, especially affecting children.

Nowadays, the WHO considers the tobacco epidemic a global challenge demanding concerted global and national action. Therefore, the WHO held a Framework Convention on Tobacco Control (WHO FCTC) containing the blueprint for coordinated global action to address one of the most significant risks to health. The FCTC follows Article 19 of the WHO Constitution and is principally a collection of effective tobacco control policies that could be adopted in different political and geographic jurisdictions. The FCTC is a framework convention/protocol approach that allows countries to proceed incrementally after they have ratified the basic treaty.

The aims of this chapter are to review the major figures about tobacco use.

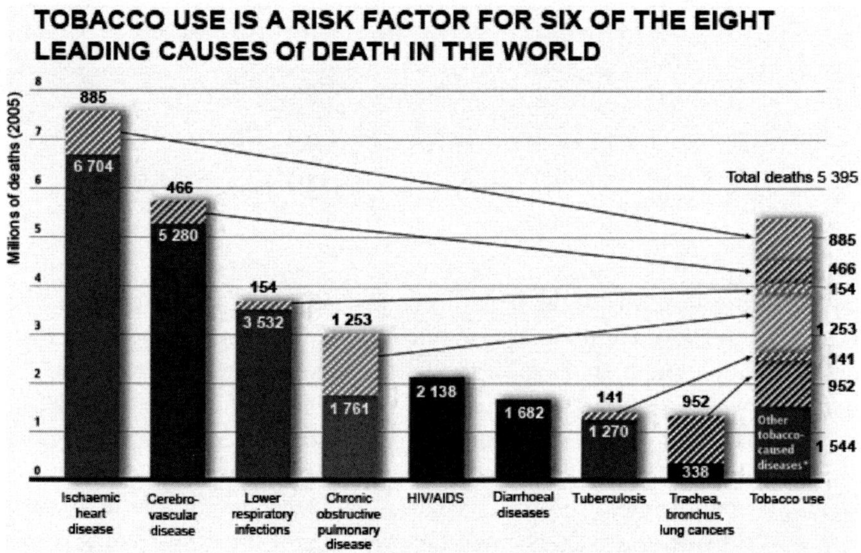

Figure 1. Tobacco use as risk factors for diseases (World Health Organisation, 2009).

THE TOBACCO EPIDEMIC

Since 1970 to 2000, world tobacco consumption has increased by over 75%, from 4.2 million tonnes in 1970 to 7.4 million tonnes of tobacco leaf equivalent in dry weight in 2000 (Food and Agriculture Organization of the United Nations, 2003). Manufactured cigarettes, together with the hand-rolled bidis consumed in South Asia, account for about 85% of all tobacco consumed worldwide. Total world cigarette consumption increased during the period 1970 to 2000 at about 2% annually. The total global prevalence in smoking is 29% (47.5% of men and 10.3% of women over 15 years of age smoke) (World Health Organization, 2003b). Consumption of tobacco products is increasing with divergent patterns (Food and Agriculture Organization of the United

Nations, 2003). Over 70% of the world total consumption, that is, about 5.3 million tonnes of tobacco leaf equivalent in dry weight, is consumed in the developing countries and the remaining 2.1 million tonnes is consumed in the developed countries. The trends are quite divergent, consumption in developed countries declined from 2.3 million tonnes in 1970 to 2.1 million tonnes in 2000 (that is, a decrease of -0.2% annually), while consumption in the developing countries increased from 2.1 million tonnes in 1970 to 5.3 million tonnes in 2000 (that is an increase of +3.1% annually). However, cigarette consumption in developed countries increased by just 10% over the period, while cigarette consumption in developing countries increased threefold over the thirty year period, with an annual growth rate of about 6%. Much of the increase in developing country consumption is accounted for by China where consumption increased from a little under 0.7 million tonnes in 1970 to 2.6 million tonnes in 2000.

Aggregate consumption in developed countries declined over the period examined by 5% in total but, taking into account the population growth, this is a rather stronger decline in consumption per capita. Among the developed countries the decline in consumption is most pronounced in North America where tobacco consumption declined steadily during the period 1970 to 2000 at an average rate of 1.3% annually (while cigarette consumption declined an average of 0.9% per annum).

In Europe consumption increased slowly up to 1990, but subsequently declined by about 2.9% annually. Despite this decline, tobacco consumption in the European Union (EU) is still higher than in 1970 by 50 000 tonnes. (Cigarette consumption in the EU experienced an increase of 1% per annum.). In Europe about 215 million people smoke, of whom 130 million are male. According to data from 25 countries, covering 60% of the population of the region, average smoking prevalence in the male population is around 34% for western European countries and 47% for eastern European countries. In the female population the prevalence is some 25% for western European countries and 20% for eastern European countries. Smoking prevalence among people aged 15–18 years is estimated at around 30%, with a slight upward trend and with no country showing a decrease in recent years. Gender differences between countries are particularly noticeable. In those over 15 years of age, boys report higher rates than girls in most of the countries in the eastern part of the region, although the gap is steadily diminishing. In Western Europe, the rates for girls are (with a few exceptions) higher than those for boys.

When data are available, they show significant differences in the prevalence of smoking between different socioeconomic groups. In the United

Kingdom, for instance, only 10% of women and 12% of men in the highest socioeconomic group are smokers, whereas in the lowest socioeconomic group the corresponding figures are more than three times higher. A strong inverse relationship is also found between the level of employment and smoking. In every country with available data, unemployed people are more likely to smoke than those who are employed. In France, smoking prevalence among unemployed males is 52%, compared with 38% for those who are employed. Overall, during the period 1970 to 2000, cigarette consumption showed a slow annual increase of about 0.4 percent. Cigarette consumption peaked at about 2000 grams per capita per year in the early 1980s and subsequently declined.

Tobacco consumption in the area of the former USSR, after a small increase to 1990 and a rapid decline during the period of transition in the early 1990s, is increasing steadily and shows a growth of 1.1% per annum during the period 1970 to 2000. In the other developed countries, including Oceania, Japan, Israel and South Africa, tobacco consumption has followed a slow decline with an average annual rate of about -0.7% during the examined period.

Even second-hand smoke may considered an epidemic. For example, in Europe it is estimated that 14% of non-smokers and 23% of smokers are exposed to other people's tobacco smoke at home on an almost daily basis, although there are great between the different countries (The Gallup Organisation, 2009). The Global Youth Tobacco Survey (Centers for Disease Control and Prevention, 2006), developed by the US Centers for Disease Prevention and Control and WHO, estimated the exposure of 13–15-year-olds to tobacco smoke in a large number of countries in the European Region. On average, exposure to second-hand smoke at home was 79%, and 84% outside home.

In the US, cigarette smoking estimates in adulthood vary between different age bands: in the 18–24 years bands it is 23.9%, in the 25–44 years bands it is 23.5%, in the 45–64 years bands it is 21.8%, and in the 65+ years band it is 10.2% (Centers for Disease Control and Prevention, 2007). The prevalence of smoking is highest among American Indians/Alaska Natives (32.4%), followed by African Americans (23.0%), whites (21.9%), Hispanics (15.2%), and Asians [excluding Native Hawaiians and other Pacific Islanders] (10.4%) (Centers for Disease Control and Prevention, 2007). When cigarette consumption is broken down by level of education and income, cigarette smoking estimates are highest for adults with a General Education Diploma (46.0%) or 9–12 years of education (35.4%), and lowest for adults with an undergraduate college degree (9.6%) or a graduate college degree (6.6%).

Furthermore, it is more common among adults who live below the poverty level (30.6%) than among those living at or above the poverty level (20.4%) (Centers for Disease Control and Prevention, 2007). When evaluating cigarette smoking by US States, the CDC estimate indicate that Kentucky (28.6%), West Virginia (25.7%), Oklahoma (25.1%), and Mississippi (25.1%) had the highest prevalence of current smokers, while smoking prevalence was lowest in Utah (9.8%), California (14.9%), and Idaho (16.8%) (Centers for Disease Control and Prevention, 2008a).

In developing countries, aggregate consumption increased by 70% over the thirty-year period, while total cigarette consumption increased in developing countries by 3.7% per annum. This is due to a large extent to developments in the two most populous countries of the world, China (where cigarette consumption increased 4.8% annually during the thirty-years period) and India (where consumption of unmanufactured tobacco products accounts for 80% of total tobacco consumption), but also due to a rapid increase in tobacco consumption observed across all developing countries.

The major factors that fuel the increase in consumption in developing countries are principally the large population and income growth (Food and Agriculture Organization of the United Nations, 2003). High income growth, coupled with high income elasticities, boosts the consumption of tobacco products in populous countries such as China, India and Brazil, thereby increasing the share of developing countries in world consumption.

Gender, Age, and Tobacco Consumption

Trends in tobacco use differ by gender. While male rates have peaked and are in slow decline, female rates are still rising. The prediction is that, while 9.3% of the female population currently smoke, this will rise to 20% by 2025 (Greaves, 2007; Samet & Yoon, 2001).

Lopez et al. (1994) created a four-stage model to explain the progression of tobacco use through populations and countries. In stage 1, smoking rates are low for both men and women, but cigarettes are increasing in popularity among men. In stage 2, countries experience a sharp increase in the prevalence of smoking among men, while women gradually begin smoking as well. In stage 3, men's rates of smoking have peaked and are starting to decline, and women's smoking begins to decrease, but at a much slower rate. In the stage 4, the decline in women's and men's smoking rates continues, but mortality due to tobacco is generally increasing among women as a result of the delay of many of tobacco's health effects.

Gender-based differences also exist for children and youth, whose tobacco use patterns may determine the shape of the epidemic for the next several decades. However, there are fewer significant gender differences in smoking as time goes by, indicating that the gender gap appears to be closing and the future of the tobacco epidemic among women may eventually grow beyond the actual estimate (Global Youth Tobacco Survey Collaborating Group, 2003).

In the US some 80% of adult smokers reportedly started smoking before the age of 18 (US Department of Health and Human Services, 1994). The WHO estimated that approximately 24% of smokers start by age 10 (World Health Organization, 2003a). In the US, approximately 3,600 young people between the ages of 12 and 17 years initiate cigarette smoking each day, and an estimated 1,100 young people become daily cigarette smokers (Substance Abuse and Mental Health Services Administration, 2007).

In Europe, according to the WHO Health Behaviour in School-aged Children study (HBSC) (Currie, Hurrelmann, Settertobulte, Smith, & Todd, 2000; Currie et al., 2004; Godeau, Rahav, & Hublet, 2004), the proportions of young people reporting having smoked rise significantly with age: from 15% for 11-year-olds to 40% for 13-year-olds and 62% for 15-year-olds. In almost half the countries and regions, these rates are at least three times higher for 13-year-olds than for 11-year-olds. Among 11-year-olds, the rates of ever having smoked are substantially higher for boys than for girls of the same age in almost all countries and regions. At age 13, however, this is true for less than half the countries and regions, with around one third having similar rates for boys and girls and more than a quarter with higher rates for girls. This trend continues in the 15-year-olds, where more girls than boys have smoked in over half the countries and regions, the difference being particularly marked in Scotland and Wales.

In contrast, across all age groups in eastern European countries and some central European countries, where the overall rates are highest, boys are more likely to have experimented with tobacco smoking. About one third of the 16% who smoke do so less than once a week (5%) with the other two thirds (11%) smoke at least once a week, 7% of whom (almost half of all smokers) smoke daily. These figures, however, hide striking age, gender and geographical differences. For all countries and regions combined, rates of weekly smoking increase with age, from 2% among 11-year-olds, to 8%

among 13-year-olds to 24% among 15-year-olds. Gender differences follow a similar pattern to those found for ever having smoked.

In 2007, 20% of high school students in the US were current cigarette smokers. There are racial/ethnic differences with approximately 23% of white, 17% of Hispanic, and 12% of African American high school students current cigarette smokers (Centers for Disease Control and Prevention, 2008b).

Initiation of smoking is influenced by education and socioeconomic status. People of higher socioeconomic status usually begin smoking at an earlier age, and males earlier than females. European research indicates that girls and boys exhibit different patterns in their reasons for smoking, such as coping with different negative emotions, enhancing friendships or co-consumption of other substances (Lambert, Hublet, Verduyckt, Maes, & Broucke, 2002). For example, peer approval positively correlates with smoking in girls more strongly than in boys, and rebelliousness and sociability indicate a propensity to smoke more in girls than in boys.

Some other factors associated with youth tobacco use include low socioeconomic status, use and approval of tobacco by peers or siblings, smoking by parents or guardians, accessibility, availability and price of tobacco products, a perception that tobacco use is normative, lack of parental support or involvement, low levels of academic achievement, lack of skills in resisting influences to use tobacco, lower self-image or self-esteem, belief in the functional benefits of tobacco use, and lack of self-efficacy in refusing offers of tobacco (US Department of Health and Human Services, 1994, 2000).

Recent genetic research indicates that there are sex differences in the metabolism of nicotine which may play a role in the trajectory of addiction, maintenance patterns and responses to cessation interventions (US Department of Health and Human Services, 2000). In addition, women have fewer successful smoking cessation attempts and more relapses than men (Osler, Prescott, Godfredsen, Hein, & Schnohr, 1999; Perkins, Donny, & Caggiula, 1991; Samet & Yoon, 2001).

TOBACCO AND HEALTH

WHO identifies tobacco smoking as the leading cause of premature illness and death in developed countries (Murray & Lopez, 1996). Globally the health costs of smoking range from about the 0.7% to 2% of the gross domestic product. In the USA, the costs of smoking are estimated to be responsible for between 6% and 10% of that country's medical care expenditures (World Health Organization, 1999). Cigarettes kill half of all lifetime users, and half of those die in middle age (35-69 years). It is currently responsible for the death of one in ten adults worldwide. Every 6.5 seconds, one tobacco user dies from a tobacco-related disease somewhere in the world (World Health Organization, 2003b). The death toll from tobacco consumption is now 4.9 million people a year. If action is not taken to curb the spread of tobacco use, annual deaths are expected to reach 8.3 million by 2030, of which more than 80% will be in developing countries (Mathers & Loncar, 2006). An estimate of global tobacco deaths calculated in 2000 shows that tobacco-related diseases killed about 100 million persons in the 20th century. If current trends persist, tobacco would kill 150 million persons in the first quarter of the 21st century and 300 million persons in the second quarter (World Health Organization, 2007a).

In Europe, the annual number of deaths attributable to the consumption of tobacco products is estimated at 1.2 million (14% of all deaths) (World Health Organisation, 1999). Of these, 700,000 occur in the countries of Central and Eastern Europe and the newly independent states (Armenia, Azerbaijan, Belarus, Georgia, Kazakhstan, Kyrgyzstan, Moldova, Russia, Tajikistan, Turkmenistan, the Ukraine, and Uzbekistan). Changes in mortality from cancer of the trachea, bronchus and lung may be used as a marker of past trends in smoking prevalence (WHO Regional Office for Europe, 2002). Since 1985, the male death rate has been slightly decreasing in the western part of Europe and has stabilized since 1995 in the countries of Central and Eastern Europe. These trends could support the view that the situation is becoming stabilized among the male population. Although lung cancer mortality is much lower in women than in men (for the region as whole, the standardized death rate for females in 1998 was 13 per 100,000 and that for males 73 per 100,000), the trends in the EU and the countries of Central and Eastern Europe are not favourable. The time lag between current smoking behaviour and manifestation of the disease points to the need for serious efforts to curb the smoking epidemic in women. Socioeconomic differences in mortality from lung cancer have been observed in all European countries for which data are available. Smoking appears to be a major factor for the difference in risk of premature death between non-manual and manual workers.

In the US, cigarette smoking remains the leading preventable cause of death (Centers for Disease Control and Prevention, 2002), accounting for approximately 1 of every 5 deaths (438,000 people) each year (Centers for Disease Control and Prevention, 2004, 2005).

Even in young people, smoking may leads to short-term health problems, including reduced lung function and shortness of breath, and greater susceptibility to and severity of respiratory illness (US Department of Health and Human Services, 1994).

WHO Policies to Reverse the Tobacco Epidemic

In May 2003, the WHO World Health Assembly adopted the WHO Framework Convention on Tobacco Control, the world's first treaty against tobacco. To expand the fight against the tobacco epidemic, WHO has introduced the MPOWER package of six policies (World Health Organization, 2008):

- Monitor tobacco use and prevention policies,
- Protect people from tobacco smoke,
- Offer help to quit tobacco use,
- Warn about the dangers of tobacco,
- Enforce bans on tobacco advertising, promotion and sponsorship, and
- Raise taxes on tobacco.

Monitor Tobacco Use and Prevention Policies

For the WHO, strong national and international monitoring is essential for the fight against the tobacco epidemic to succeed. Data from monitoring are necessary to ensure the success of the five other policy interventions in the MPOWER package. Comprehensive monitoring informs the leaders of governments and the society how the tobacco epidemic harms their countries, and helps them allocate tobacco control resources where they are most needed and will be most effective.

For the WHO, effective monitoring systems must track several indicators, including the prevalence of tobacco use, the impact of policy interventions; and tobacco industry marketing, promotion and lobbying. Monitoring programmes need to provide overarching as well as specific information on the tobacco epidemic. These include surveys on tobacco use prevalence and consumption levels by age, sex, income and other demographic subdivisions, both nationally and by province or region. The effectiveness of local and national tobacco prevention programmes must also be closely assessed.

Protect People from Tobacco Smoke

The WHO considers smoke-free environments necessary to prevent hazards to health and to help smokers who want to quit. Furthermore, some international bodies such as the Conference of the Parties to the Framework Convention (World Health Organization, 2007b), the WHO International Agency for Research on Cancer (World Health Organization/International Agency for Research on Cancer IARC, 2002), the US Surgeon General (US Department of Health and Human Services, 2006) and the United Kingdom Scientific Committee on Tobacco and Health (Scientific Committee on Tobacco and Health, 2004) all are in agreement that second-hand smoke exposure contributes to a range of potentially lethal diseases.

Legislation mandating smoke-free public places may encourage families to make their homes smoke-free (Borland et al., 2006).

For the WHO, complete prohibition of smoking in all indoor environments is the only intervention that effectively protects people from the harm of second-hand smoke (Office of Environmental Health Hazard Assessment, 1997; World Health Organization/International Agency for Research on Cancer IARC, 2002). Full enforcement of smoke-free laws is critical to establishing their credibility, especially immediately following their enactment (WHO Tobacco Free Initiative, 2004). WHO recommends a step-by-step process as the most effective method to create smoke-free environments (WHO Tobacco Free Initiative, 2004). To begin, governments should prepare educational campaigns for the public and business communities about the dangers of second-hand smoke. After building widespread support for smoke-free spaces, legislation should be drafted and submitted for public comment. Once this groundwork has been done, governments need to maintain strong public and political support for smoke-free places, and then pass comprehensive legislation that includes clear penalties for violations as well as effective enforcement policies. Once enacted, governments must maintain strong support for the law through aggressive and uniform enforcement that achieves high compliance levels.

Offer Help to Quit Tobacco Use

As with people dependent on any addictive drug, tobacco users may benefit from help and support to overcome their dependence. The health-care systems of countries hold the primary responsibility for treating tobacco dependence. For the WHO, three types of treatment should be included in any tobacco prevention effort: 1) tobacco cessation advice incorporated into primary health-care services; 2) easily accessible and free quit lines; and 3) access to low-cost pharmacological therapy.

Integrating tobacco cessation into primary health care and other routine medical visits provides the health-care system with opportunities to remind users that tobacco harms their health and that of others around them. Advice from health-care practitioners can greatly increase abstinence rates (Fiore, 2008).

Warn About the Dangers of Tobacco

Despite conclusive evidence on the dangers of tobacco, relatively few tobacco users worldwide fully grasp its health risks. The extreme addictiveness of tobacco and the full range of health dangers have not been adequately explained to the public. Thus, comprehensive warnings about the dangers of tobacco are critical to changing its image, especially among adolescents and young adults. People need to associate tobacco with its extreme addictiveness and dangerous health consequences, and to see it as socially undesirable and negative. All this can be achieved through anti-tobacco advertising campaigns in all forms of media to publicize the full extent of tobacco's dangers. Anti-tobacco advertising campaigns should also speak about protecting families, especially children, from the dangers of second-hand smoke.

Warnings on cigarette packages may also have an effect (Hammond, Fong, McNeill, Borland, & Cummings, 2006). Tobacco manufacturers have always used packaging as a platform to reinforce brand loyalty and users' perceived self-image, particularly among young people. Pack warnings reduce this marketing effect.

Enforce Bans on Tobacco Advertising, Promotion and Sponsorship

Marketing and promotion increase tobacco sales and creates obstacles that blunt tobacco control efforts. For example, widespread tobacco advertising "normalizes" tobacco use. Some national-level studies before and after advertising bans found a decline in tobacco consumption (Economics

Operational Research Division. (EORD) Department of Health (UK), 1992; Jha & Chaloupka, 1999; World Bank, 2003). A ban on marketing and promotion is a powerful weapon against the tobacco epidemic. To be effective, bans must be complete and apply to all marketing and promotional categories (Saffer & Chaloupka, 2000; WHO Tobacco Free Initiative, 2004).

Raise Taxes on Tobacco

Increasing the price of tobacco through higher taxes is the single most effective way to decrease consumption and encourage tobacco users to quit (WHO Tobacco Free Initiative, 2004).

References

Borland RM, Yong HH, Cummings KM, et al.: Determinants and consequences of smoke-free homes: findings from the International Tobacco Control (ITC) Four Country Survey. *Tobacco Control* 15 (Suppl. 3):iii42–iii50, 2006.

Centers for Disease Control and Prevention: Annual smoking-attributable mortality, years of potential life lost, and economic costs—United States, 1995–1999. *MMWR Morb. Mortal. Wkly. Rep.* 51:300-303, 2002.

Centers for Disease Control and Prevention: National Center for Health Statistics; health, United States, 2004 with chartbook on trends in the health of Americans. *Hyattsville: US Department of Health and Human Services,* CDC, 2004.

Centers for Disease Control and Prevention: Annual smoking-attributable mortality, years of potential life lost, and productivity losses—United States, 1997–2001. *MMWR Morb. Mortal Wkly Re*p. 54:625–628, 2005.

Centers for Disease Control and Prevention. (2006). Global Youth Tobacco Survey. Retrieved August 6th, 2006, from http://www.cdc.gov/tobacco/global/gyts/GYTS_factsheets.htm

Centers for Disease Control and Prevention: Cigarette Smoking Among Adults—United States, 2006. *MMWR Morb. Mortal Wkly Rep.* 56:1157-1161, 2007.

Centers for Disease Control and Prevention: State-specific prevalence of cigarette smoking among adults and quitting among persons aged 18–35

Years—United States, 2006. *MMWR Morb. Mortal Wkly Rep.* 56:993-996, 2008a.

Centers for Disease Control and Prevention: Cigarette use among high school students—United States, 1991–2007. *MMWR Morb. Mortal Wkly Rep.* 57:686–688, 2008b.

Currie C, Hurrelmann K, Settertobulte W, et al. (eds.): Health and health behaviour among young people: international report. Copenhagen, WHO Regional Office for Europe, 2000.

Currie C, Roberts C, Morgan A, et al. (eds.): Young people's health in context: international report from the HBSC 2001/02 survey. Copenhagen, WHO Regional Office for Europe, 2004.

Economics Operational Research Division. (EORD) Department of Health (UK): Effect of tobacco advertising on tobacco sponsorship: a discussion document reviewing the evidence. London: Department of Health, 1992.

Fiore MC. (2008). Treating tobacco use and dependence: a public health service clinical practice guideline: 2008 Update. Retrieved December 16th, 2007, from http://www.ncbi.nlm.nih.gov/books/bv.fcgi? rid=hstat2. chapter.28163

Food and Agriculture Organization of the United Nations: Projections of tobacco production, consumption and trade to the year 2010. Rome: FAO, 2003.

Global Youth Tobacco Survey Collaborating Group: Differences in worldwide tobacco use by gender: findings from the Global Youth Tobacco Survey. *Journal of School Health* 73:207, 2003.

Godeau E, Rahav G, Hublet A: Tobacco smoking, in Young people's health in context: international report from the HBSC 2001/02 survey. Edited by Currie C, Roberts C, Morgan A, et al. Copenhagen, WHO Regional Office for Europe, 2004.

Greaves L: Sifting the evidence: gender and global tobacco. Geneva: World Health Organization, 2007.

Guindon GE, Boisclair D: Past, current and future trends in tobacco use. Washington, DC: The World Bank, 2003.

Hammond D, Fong GT, McNeill A, et al.: Effectiveness of cigarette warning labels in informing smokers about the risks of smoking: findings from the Internati*onal Tobacco Control (ITC) Four Country Survey.* Tobacco Control 15 (Suppl. 3):iii19–iii25, 2006.

Jha P, Chaloupka FJ: Curbing the epidemic: governments and the economics of tobacco control. Washington, DC: World Bank, 1999.

Lambert M, Hublet A, Verduyckt P, et al.: Gender differences in smoking in young people. Brussels: Flemish Institute for Health Promotion, 2002.

Lopez AD, Collishaw NE, Piha T: A descriptive model of the cigarette epidemic in developed countries. *Tobacco Control* 3:242-247, 1994.

Mathers CD, Loncar D: Projections of global mortality and burden of disease from 2002 to 2030. *PLoS Med.* 3:e442, 2006.

Murray CJL, Lopez AD: The global burden of diseases: a comprehensive assessment of mortality and disability from diseases, injuries and risk factors in 1990 and projected to 2020. (Global Burden of Disease and Injury series, Vol. II). Cambridge: Harvard School of Public Health on behalf of the World Health Organization and the World Bank, 1996.

Novotny TE, Mamudu HM: Progression of tobacco control policies: lessons from the United States and implications for global action. Washington, DC: The World Bank, 2008.

Office of Environmental Health Hazard Assessment: Health effects of exposure to environmental tobacco smoke. Sacramento: *Environmental Protection Agency,* 1997.

Osler M, Prescott E, Godfredsen N, et al.: Gender and determinants of smoking cessation: a longitudinal study. *Prev. Med.* 29:57-62, 1999.

Perkins KA, Donny E, Caggiula A: Sex differences in nicotine effects and self-administration: human and animal evidence. *Nicotine & Tobacco Research* 1:301-315, 1991.

Saffer H, Chaloupka F: The effect of tobacco advertising bans on tobacco consumption. *J. Health Econ.* 19:1117-1137, 2000.

Samet JM, Yoon SY (eds.): Women and the tobacco epidemic: challenges for the 21st century. Geneva, World Health Organization, 2001.

Scientific Committee on Tobacco and Health: Secondhand Smoke: Review of evidence since 1998. Update of evidence on health effects of secondhand smoke. London: *Scientific Committee on Tobacco and Health,* 2004.

Substance Abuse and Mental Health Services Administration: National survey on drug use and health. NSDUH Series H-27, DHHS Publication No. SMA 05–4061. Rockville: Office of Applied Studies, 2007.

The Gallup Organisation: Survey on Tobacco. Analytical report. Flash Eurobarometer 253. Budapest: The Gallup Organisation, 2009.

U.S. Department of Health EaW: Smoking and Health: Report of the Advisory Committee of the Surgeon General of the Public Health Service. Princeton: D. Van Nostrand Co., 1964.

US Department of Health and Human Services: Preventing tobacco use among young people: a report of the Surgeon General. Atlanta: US Department of

Health and Human Services, Public Health Service, Centers for Disease Control and Prevention, National Center for Chronic Disease Prevention and Health Promotion, Office on Smoking and Health, 1994.

US Department of Health and Human Services: Reducing tobacco use: a report of the Surgeon General. Atlanta: : US Department of Health and Human Services, Centers for Disease Control and Prevention, Coordinating Center for Health Promotion, National Center for Chronic Disease Prevention and Health Promotion, Office on Smoking and Health, 2000.

US Department of Health and Human Services: The health consequences of involuntary exposure to tobacco smoke: a report of the Surgeon General. Atlanta: US Department of Health and Human Services, Centers for Disease Control and Prevention, Coordinating Center for Health Promotion, National Center for Chronic Disease Prevention and Health Promotion, Office on Smoking and Health, 2006.

WHO Regional Office for Europe: The European Health Report 2002. Copenhagen: *World Health Organization,* 2002.

WHO Tobacco Free Initiative: Building blocks for tobacco control: a handbook. Geneva: *World Health Organization,* 2004.

World Bank. (2003). Public health at a glance – Tobacco control. Why is reducing use of tobacco a priority? Retrieved September 19th, 2009, from http://siteresources.worldbank.org/INTPHAAG/Resources/AAGTobacControlEngv46-03.pdf

World Health Organisation: HEALTH21: the health for all policy framework for the WHO European Region. Copenhagen: WHO Regional Office for Europe, 1999.

World Health Organisation. (2009). Tobacco Free Initiative (TFI). Graphs. Retrieved September 19th, 2009, from http://www.who.int/tobacco/mpower/graphs/en/index.html

World Health Organization: Confronting the epidemic: a global agenda for tobacco control research. Geneva: Research for International Tobacco Control and the World Health Organization, 1999.

World Health Organization: Tobacco and the rights of the child. Geneva: World Health Organization, 2001.

World Health Organization: Gender, health and tobacco. Geneva: WHO, Department of Gender and Women's Health, 2003a.

World Health Organization: World Health Report 2003: shaping the future. Geneva: World Health Organization, 2003b.

World Health Organization: A WHO / The Union monograph on TB and tobacco control: joining efforts to control two related global epidemics. Geneva: World Health Organization, 2007a.

World Health Organization. (2007b). Conference of the Parties to the WHO Framework Convention on Tobacco Control. Retrieved September 20th, 2009, from http://www.who.int/gb/fctc/PDF/cop2/FCTC_COP2_17P-en.pdf

World Health Organization: WHO report on the global tobacco epidemic, 2008 The MPOWER package. Geneva: World Health Organization, 2008.

World Health Organization. (2009). Tobacco facts. Retrieved September 20th, 2009, from http://www.who.int/tobacco/mpower/ tobacco_facts/en/ index. html

World Health Organization/International Agency for Research on Cancer IARC: Tobacco smoke and involuntary smoking: summary of data reported and evaluation. Geneva: World Health Organization, 2002.

Chapter 2

SMOKING AS A RISK FACTOR FOR SUICIDE

ABSTRACT

Cigarette smoking is associated with an increased risk for suicide (ideation, plans and actions). However, findings regarding this relationship are not yet consistent. Despite the fact that the prevalence of smoking is higher in suicidal individuals, it is not clear that smoking itself (or the effect of nicotine on brain function) is directly involved in suicidality or whether other factors associated with both suicide and smoking are implicated in this relationship. Indeed it has been found that several suicide risk factors are more common among current smokers than among those who have never smoked.

We identified the main hypotheses for explaining this association, focusing on the effect of nicotine exposure on the neurobiological system as a causal mechanism influencing suicidality in long-term smokers. Then we examined the association between tobacco and psychological problems (such as depression, alcohol use and schizophrenia) as possible determinants of an increased risk of suicide in smokers. Finally we reviewed the magnitude of smoking during adolescence.

Despite the large literature available, the findings are not yet consistent. Most likely, several factors contribute to the increased rate of suicidal behavior in current smokers. Future research is required to provide guidance in suicide prevention among smokers.

INTRODUCTION

The 2007 National Health Interview Survey indicates that approximately 19.8% (43.4 million) U.S. adults were current cigarette smokers in 2007 (CDC, 2007). Cigarette smoking is probably the leading preventable cause of premature death. It was estimated that, each year in USA, 443,000 people die prematurely as a result of smoking (CDC, 2008).

According to WHO data, approximately one million people died in 2008 by suicide (WHO, 2008), and suicide is now among the three leading causes of death among those aged 15-44 years for both sexes. An important branch of suicidology (defined as the discipline devoted to the scientific study of suicide and its prevention) is involved in identifying the predictors and the causes of suicidality. Unfortunately, it is often a difficult task because the causes of suicide are multifactorial with genetic and biologic vulnerability, environmental factors, psychological pain, mental and physical illnesses, substance abuse and personality disorders each playing a role (Mann, 1998). Therefore, it is not always easy to establish which variables independently contribute to the occurrence of suicidal behavior. However, several psychosocial, demographic and behavioral factors have been identified, including age, marital status, life events, social support, major depressive episodes, dysthymia, schizophrenia, alcohol use and smoking (Bernal, 2007; Casey, 2006).

Research has identified a strong relationship between tobacco smoking and suicidal behavior. In general, cigarette smoking is more frequent among people with suicidal ideation than among the general population (Malone, 2003; Kessler, 2007). More specifically, post-mortem studies of suicides has found that smokers are overrepresented (Angst, 1998). Moreover, suicides are more likely to have high blood and urine levels of nicotine and cotine in contrast to those dying from other causes (Benwell, 1990; Kochi, 2005; Moriya, 2005, 2007).

A link between smoking and suicide has been reported in several studies, and smoking has been suggested as a possible risk factor for suicide, but the research findings are not completely consistent. Although the prevalence of smoking is higher in suicidal people, it is less clear that smoking itself (or the effect of nicotine on brain function) is directly involved in increasing the level of suicidality. Other factors associated with both suicide and smoking may be implicated in this relationship. For example, it has been found that several well-established risk factors for suicide, such as depressive moods, alcohol use and abuse, impulsivity, low emotional control, social isolation and schizophrenia, are more common among current than smokers than among those who have never smoked.

The main interpretations proposed to explain the association between smoking and suicide may be summarized in two opposed models. The first supports a causal influence of smoking on suicidality. It is based on evidence of the effect of nicotine exposure on human biochemistry. Nicotine has direct effects on the central nervous system, and these effects might be responsible for, or mediate, the link between smoking and suicidality in two different ways. The direct neurological effect of nicotine (or other tobacco components) may induce suicidal behavior or, alternatively, the central effect of nicotine may induce behavioral or mood alterations which in turn may act as mediators between smoking and suicide risk (see below).

An interesting and alternative approach endeavors to identify whether smoking habits precede (and so possibly cause) suicidal behavior or some of the possible suicide precursors (especially depression) (Choi, 1997; Breslau, 2004; Li-Tzy, 1999; Goodman, 2000). Related to this is the question of whether stopping smoking reduces the risk of suicide or suicide risk factors (Leistykow, 2003; Mino, 2000; Khaled, 2009). For example, Mino and colleagues evaluated mental status six months and one years after cessation of smoking and found a gradual improvement in physical health, perceived stress and family life satisfaction. An indirect confirmation of this first hypothesis is the finding that former smokers did not have higher rates of psychological disorders or suicidal behavior compared to non-smokers (Degenhardt, 2001). Only current smoking, and not previous smoking, is linked to increased suicidal behavior (Miller, 2000a, 2000b; Leistikow, 1999; Hemenway, 1993; Breslau, 2005).

The second possible interpretation stems from the observation that current smoking is correlated with many other risk factors for suicide. Various conditions (behavioral, psychiatric, and life events) and variables associated with smoking are also suicide risk factors, and they may act as potential mediators to produce the association between smoking and suicide (Boden, 2008; Kessler, 2008; Hintikka, 2009; Breslau, 1998). Therefore, the genetic, psychological, environmental and other risk factors for suicide may explain the association between smoking and suicide. In this view, cigarette smoking is independently correlated with traits predisposing to suicide, and smoking may be considered to be only an indicator, a useful marker, for an increased risk of suicidal behavior. Its effect on suicidality may not be direct and causal. Alternatively, specific psychological factors may produce an increased susceptibility to tobacco use, and they may act or contribute to the association between smoking and suicide.

Some authors also suggest that the association between smoking and suicide is the result of methodological artifacts and errors of interpretation of the data. For example, in some epidemiological studies, there are inadequate controls for psychological factors (Miller, 2000a; Kessler, 2007). Correcting for psychological variables (such as diagnosis, alcohol or drug use and abuse, experience of trauma, personality traits and poor emotional control) results in a reduction or elimination of the association between smoking and suicide (Boden, 2008; Hemmingsson, 2003; Patten, 2003; McGee, 2005).

Criticism regarding the possibility that the correlation between smoking and suicide implies causation was offered by Smith and colleagues (1992). They analyzed data from Multiple Risk Factor Intervention Trial (MRFIT), a study involving 361,662 men, with a 12-year follow-up. They found a strong dose-response association between smoking and completed suicide but also between smoking and homicide. They interpreted this as evidence against the biological plausibility of a causal interpretation of the smoking-suicide association.

The decreased risk of suicidal behavior may be a consequence of smoking cessation. There are two different situations associated with this. Stopping smoking may gradually reduce the level of depressive mood and may improve mental health and, as a side effect, decrease suicidality. However, research indicates that, in the first stages of smoking cessation, some individuals (especially those with a history of depression) may develop depressive symptoms and, occasionally, a major depressive episode (Covey, 1997; Glassman, 1988; Tsoh, 2000), along with increased suicidality. In additon, the emergence of depressive symptoms is associated with a failure in smoking cessation. The risk of developing a major depressive episode (and consequently an increase in suicidality) during the first months without cigarettes is partly due to suspension symptoms. In nicotine dependent people, a sudden interruption or reduction in nicotine intake may bring about withdrawal symptoms, including insomnia, irritability, anger, difficulty in concentration and restlessness, as well as dysphoria, depression and anxiety (APA, 2000). The emergence of depressive symptoms may extend beyond the usual withdrawal period (2-4 weeks) (Covey, 1997). Second, there is evidence about that two products used in smoking cessation programs may enhance depression and cause suicidality. The US Food and Drug Administration (FDA) has issued warnings about the possibility that depressed mood, suicidal ideation and suicidal behavior can occur in patients, with and without a psychiatric history, who attempt to quit smoking using Verenicline or Bupropion (FDA, 2005, 2008).

Studies of adolescents are important. The onset of daily smoking rarely occurs after the age of 25 (Breslau, 2001). Those who start smoking before the age of 16 are 1.6 times more likely to become nicotine dependent than those who start smoking at an older age (Breslau, 1993; Martinez-Ortega, 2008). Adolescence is considered to be a time of high risk for both suicide and smoking. Adolescents are more vulnerable to emotional perturbations and distress and, therefore, are at an increased risk of suicide. Among adolescents suicide is the third leading cause of death.

Menti and coworkers (2007) found that smoking was 10-times more frequent among young suicide attempters (age 9-20) than among controls. According to The Youth Risk Behavior Surveillance, 14.5% of the students had seriously considered attempting suicide, 11.3% of students had made a plan about how they would attempt suicide and 6.9% of students had attempted suicide one or more times during the 12 months before the survey (Eaton, 2008).

Around 20.0% of students currently smoke (Eaton, 2008). Initially, smoking during youth is limited to social situations. Gradually a dependence is established and, at the same time, the number of cigarettes smoked increases (Patton, 1998). In this context, depression seems to be a predictor for smoking initiation (Patton, 1998). On the other hand, other research demonstrates that, during adolescence, tobacco smoking is associated with an increased risk for the subsequent onset of depressed mood (Li-Tzy, 1999). Brown and colleagues (1996) conducted a prospective study to establish whether adolescent smokers are more likely to develop a major depressive episode in the follow-up period (12 months) or whether those with previous psychiatric disorders, such as depression, are more likely to develop a smoking habit in the following year. Their findings indicated that the presence of a major depressive disorder (but not other psychiatric disorders) was a risk factor for beginning cigarette smoking, while smoking at the onset of the study was a predictor for the development of depression. This bidirectionality between smoking and depression may support the above-mentioned hypothesis of a common vulnerability to both, or it may support the self-medication hypothesis and the possibility that same psychosocial problems associated with smoking risk are also associated with an increased susceptibility to depressive mood.

In this chapter, we review the effects of nicotine exposure on the neurobiological system and research on the association between nicotine consumption and different psychiatric disorders. In addition, we evaluate the possible implication of smoking cessation on the neurobiological system and on suicide.

1. Nicotine Biochemical Interactions and Suicide

Nicotine is a potent psychoactive drug with both acute and chronic central nervous system effects, including influences on mood. In particular, the interaction between nicotine and the serotonergic system is of particular clinical importance given the central role of these receptors in anxiety and depression-related illness. In this biochemical context, the difficulty in determining what is the real role of tobacco on suicidality is due to the fact that nicotine has a double effect in regulating the serotonergic system. Specifically, the acute administration of nicotine induces the release of 5-HT (Ribeiro, 1993; Kenny, 2001), while chronic smoking reduces 5-HT1A receptor gene expression and the sensitivity of serotonin receptors in the frontal cortex (Kenny, 2001), reduces serotonin reuptake (Benwell, 1990), and ultimately diminishes serotonergic transmission. The immediate antidepressant-like effect of nicotine may relieve feelings of stress, depression, anger and dysphoria. This effect is, therefore, ill-suited to explain a direct relationship between smoking and suicide. The use of nicotine as a form of self-medication may, however, explain the association between depression and smoking.

On the other hand, long-term smoking may cause lower brain serotonin function that, in turn, is associated with an increased susceptibility to suicide. The increased anxiety and negative affect observed in smokers may also be relevant. Consistent with these results, research has identified differences between suicides and control groups in markers of central nervous system serotonin function such as lower central 5-HT activity (Mann, 2002, 2003; Kamali, 2001). Lower platelet 5-HT (blood platelets are often used as a limited peripheral model for central 5-HT neural function) has been associated with suicidal behavior in psychotic and non-psychotic depressed patients (Muck-Seler et al, 1996; Pivac et al, 1997) and in patients with first episode of psychosis (Marcinko et al, 2007). Another relevant biochemical aspect is monoamine oxidase (MAO) activity. The influence of smoking on MAO may play a role in the psychopathology of depression and suicide in smokers (Whitfield, 2000). MAO activity seems to be lower in current smokers than former smokers and those who have never smoked (Merlin, 1995; Berlin, 1995). MAO activity has been shown to be inversely associated with impulsive behavior, and it is also lower in suicidal patients as compared to nonsuicidal depressed patients and healthy controls (Roggenbach, 2006; Stålenheim, 2001; Verkes, 1998).

McGee and coworkers (2005) found that tobacco smoking does not appear to elevate the risk of later suicidal ideation in adolescents. However, they did not take into account the level of nicotine dependence. Heatherton et al. (1989) found that those individuals who smoke soon after waking up are highly nicotine-dependent. The likelihood of suicidality is known to be correlated with the amount of smoking via lowered serotonergic function. When measuring levels of CSF 5-HIAA (5-hydroxyindoleacetic acid concentrations in the cerebrospinal fluid) in depressed subjects, Malone and colleagues (2003) found that CSF 5-HIAA levels were negatively correlated with the amount of cigarette smoking, but were not related to suicide attempter status. Furthermore, the number of cigarettes smoked correlated positively with aggression scores. Thus, according to Malone et al., nicotine may have both biological and behavioral effects in the brain that increase the probability of suicidal behaviour in depressed patients. As also shown in previous studies (Breslau et al, 2005), early morning smoking and a high number of cigarettes smoked per day, as opposed to moderate smoking, are valid indicators of nicotine dependence. Therefore, nicotine dependence might explain the finding of an increased risk for suicidal attempts, but not suicidal ideation, in adolescent heavy daily smoking.

Audrain and coworkers (2004) followed 15-year-old students enrolled in public schools in northern Virginia and provided the first evidence for an association of the DRD2 A1 allele with smoking progression among adolescents and a relationship between the adolescents' response to their first exposure to nicotine and their subsequent risk for nicotine dependence. (The SLC6A3 polymorphism was not associated with smoking progression.)

2. COMORBIDITY

Research investigating the association between nicotine consumption and various psychiatric disorders has shown that nicotine dependence is much more prevalent among psychiatric patients than in the general population. People with mental illness are about twice as likely to smoke (Lasser, 2000; Poirier, 2002; Kessler, 2007; Grant, 2004). Although the mechanisms that influence this association are unclear, this could account for the high rate of suicidal behavior among smokers. Several possible explanations have been considered for the association between psychiatric disorders and smoking. Nicotine may have a direct deleterious effect on mental health status (i.e., a nicotine central effect) and generate depression. Alternatively, pre-existing mental health problems may lead to smoking, or there may be a shared, possibly genetic, etiology. Whatever the cause, the relationship between tobacco and problems such as depression, schizophrenia, and alcohol and substance use have to be considered in the association of an increased risk of suicide in smokers.

Research suggests that smokers are more likely to be depressed than nonsmokers (Pedersen, 2009; Murphy, 2003), and this association between smoking and depression may be particularly important in the genesis of suicidal pathways in smokers. Regarding the possibility that major depression and psychotic disorders may play a causal role in beginning smoking, this may reflect the use of smoking for self-medication. The acute chemical impact of nicotine may improve mood and reduce psychological symptoms such as dysphoria, anxiety, stress and anger and enhance attention and improve cognitive performance (Glassman, 1990; Xu, 2007; Kassel, 1997; Balfour, 2000). Moreover, the antidepressant effect of tobacco components may explain why depressed and other psychiatric patients find it more difficult to stop smoking and why there are an increase likelihood that they become heavy smokers (Murphy et al, 2003), and why some (but not all) studies report that depressive symptoms predict the development of smoking onset (Hemmingsson, 2003; Breslau, 1998; Goodman, 2000; Murphy et al, 2003), or that smoking at baseline does not predict following depression (Murphy et al, 2003). Murphy and coworkers (2003) studied the incidence of depression in cohorts of smokers and non-smokers over a 40-year period (1952-1970, 1970-1992). Over the years, the proportion of smokers declined, and the association between smoking and depressive mood was lower in 1952 and 1970, but strong in 1992. It seems that the increased awareness of the unhealthy effect of tobacco had resulted in reducing the number of smokers but, on the other hand, it selected a group of new smokers and those who persisted in smoking. This generational change suggests a psychopathologic origin (or component) in smoking initiation and continuation (Breslau, 2001). A similar observation can be made regarding the prominent abuse of cigarettes in schizophrenic patients (de Leon & Diaz, 2005).

Through dopamine release and raising dopamine levels in the prefrontal cortex and the nucleus accumbens (Dalack, 1998), nicotine may be used to manage negative symptoms (Smith, 2002). Nicotine helps reduce the extrapyramidal side effects of neuroleptics (Poirier, 2002; Yang, 2002; Goff, 1992) and reduce cognitive deficits (Adler, 1998). It is possible that genetic factors influence the genesis of both smoking and depression, and a genetic susceptibility/component to both smoking (Li, 2003; Lerman, 2003) and depression (Sullivan, 2000) has been demonstrated. Several researchers have propose that common factors, probably genetic, may predispose people to the development of both nicotine dependence and major depression (Kenneth, 1993; Breslaw, 1993; Kendler, 1993). Furthemore, it has been found that genetic subgroups of depressed patients with a specific variation in dopamine receptor genes are also more predisposed to begin smoking (Lerman, 1998), suggesting a genetic overlap between smoking and depression. On the other hand, depression may simply reinforce the effect of DRD2 A1 allelic variants (which induce lower endogenous dopamine activity) on smoking progression (Audrian-Mcgoven, 2004).

Alcohol abuse and smoking are also associated, and there is a general smoking and substance use/abuse comorbidity. Alcohol use is more frequent in smokers than in non-smokers (Degenhardt, 2001; Harrison, 2008; Leon, 2007; John, 2003; Miller, 2000b), and alsohol use and misuse is positively associated with suicidal ideation and deliberate self-harm (McCloud, 2004; Sher, 2006a; Cherpitel, 2004). Incidentally, alcohol abuse influences serotonergic metabolism and increases impulsivity and aggressive behavior (Sher, 2006b). Thus, its effect on suicidality in smokers may be a result of synergic effects.

Regarding the possibility that a positive association between alcohol and smoking alone may explain the link between smoking and suicide, Hemmingsson and Kriebel (2003) examined a longitudinal cohort study of 49,323 Swedish men to establish whether smoking at age 18–20 was related to suicide mortality during 26 years of follow-up and whether this relationship was attributable to an increased prevalence of indicators of poor mental well-being and alcohol use among the smokers. The suicides occurring during the 26-year follow-up period were linked with previous/early smoking status but, when the suicide risk was adjusted for the set of risk factors measured at age 18-20 and for a diagnosis of alcoholism during the follow-up, very little evidence of elevated suicide risk among the smokers remained. Hemmingsson and Kriebel concluded that the increased risk of suicide among smokers was almost entirely explained by the increased prevalence of heavy alcohol consumption and low mental well-being among smokers.

3. Personality, Smoking and Suicide

As mentioned above, it is not clear whether cigarette smoking *per se* increases suicidality or whether other smoking-associated factors intervene. One possibility is that the personality of the smoker makes the individual prone to suicidal behavior. The impulsivity and increased distressed behavior among smokers reported in the literature may partly account for their proneness to engage in suicidal behavior. In this view, smoking, heavy drinking, drug use, and other risky behavior represent what Shneidman called *subintentioned suicide* (Shneidman, 1985), perhaps resulting from an unconscious death wish. Ellis and Trumpower (2008) found that people reporting suicidal ideation were more likely to report risky health-related behavior (especially cigarette smoking, drinking and other substance-related involvement). This association was found even after controlling for depression.

Smokers are also more likely to have higher levels of impulsivity and aggressive behavior (Angst, 1998; Tanskanen, 1998). This may be due to the effect of nicotine on serotonergic activity that could predispose susceptible individuals to impulsive and aggressive behavior and, in turn, to suicide attempts (Horesh, 1997). Whatever the genesis, impulsive/aggressive traits are correlated with suicide attempts independently of psychiatric diagnosis. Across diagnostic categories, patients who attempted suicide have an elevated lifetime trait of aggression and impulsivity (Mann, 1999; Oquedo, 2004), and impulsivity contributes to the long-term risk for suicide (Maser, 2002).

4. Smoking and Suicide: Is Smoking a Causal or a Casual Associated Factor?

a. Studies that have Investigated a Direct Relationship between Smoking and Suicide

Tanskanen et al. (1998) studied a sample of 1,217 psychiatric patients (56% female and 44% male) in whom schizophrenia was the most common psychiatric diagnosis (33%) followed by affective disorder (29%), personality disorder (11%), dysthymia (8%) and anxiety disorder (8%). Twenty-four percent of the men and 26% of the women had attempted suicide at least once. Current smokers were defined as those who smoked at least one cigarette per day. The results showed that the rate of previous suicide attempts was significantly higher for current smokers than for nonsmokers, both for men and women.

They performed two multiple logistic regression analyses to estimate the adjusted odds ratios with 95% confidence intervals for current smoking and other possible predictors: sex, age, marital status, education, income level, employment status, psychiatric diagnosis (involving five dummy variables), alcohol drinking habits, and level of depression. In the first regression, severe depression, current smoking, male gender and anxiety disorder were associated with previous suicide attempts and entered the model in this order as significant predictors. In the second regression, severe depression, schizophrenia, female gender, current smoking and major affective disorder were associated with suicidal ideation. The authors suggested that depression could be the "third factor" linking smoking to suicidal behavior. It is known that nicotine use can provoke depression (Glassman, 1993) but, on the other hand, people with depressive symptoms find nicotine to be an effective self-medication and, in some individuals, nicotine may act as an antidepressant (Salin-Pascual et al, 1996).

Two Studies with a Large Sample

Two large-scale studies published in 2000, tried to clarify the association between smoking and suicide. A prospective study of 50,000 American men, followed up prospectively for 8 years, found a dose-response relationship between smoking and suicide. Men were characterized according to their smoking status as never smokers, current smokers or former smokers. Current smokers were characterized as smoking 1 to 14 or 15 or more cigarettes per day. Eighty-two members of the cohort committed suicide in the 8-year period. Smokers were more likely than nonsmokers to be unmarried, to be less physically active, to drink alcohol and drink heavily, to consume coffee, and to develop cancer. These tendencies were most pronounced in heavy smokers and least pronounced in former smokers. Compared with never-smokers, heavy smokers were at increased risk for suicide. The risk of suicide increased with the number of cigarettes smoked daily: current smokers of 15 or more cigarettes per day had more than 4 times the risk of suicide compared with never-smokers. The suicide risk among former smokers was intermediate between the risks among never and current smokers.

One possible interpretation of these results is that smokers and nonsmokers differ on many characteristics related to the risk of suicide. Depression (Kendler et al, 1993), schizophrenia (Lohr & Flynn, 1992; De

Leon et al, 1995), alcohol and illicit drug use (Istavan & Matarazzo, 1984), suicidal ideation and suicide attempts (Tanskanen et al, 1998), developing cancer, not being married, and otherwise being socially isolated are all risk factors for suicide that are more common among smokers than among nonsmokers. Compared with nonsmokers, smokers also tend to act out hostility and have obsessional traits and anxiety (Chiles, Benjamin & Cahn, 1990).

Four possible explanations for the smoking-suicide connection have been proposed: (1) depression is a common antecedent of suicide and a condition that leads to smoking as a form of self-medication; (2) smoking alters brain chemistry, leading to depression, which increases the risk of suicide; (3) smoking leads to malignant disease, such as cancer, which increases the risk of suicide; and (4) smoking is associated with other characteristics that predispose individuals to suicide, such as low self-esteem.

Miller et al. (2000) examined the relation between cigarette smoking and suicide in a cohort study of 300,000 male American soldiers. The authors took into account a number of potential confounders, including age, race, alcohol intake, marital status, education, military rank, and physical activity. During the follow-up period, there were 113 suicides in the cohort. Miller et al. found that smokers were more likely than nonsmokers to be white, drink heavily, be married, be less educated, be of enlisted rank, and exercise less often. Except for marital status, these tendencies were more extreme in heavy smokers than in light smokers. The suicide rate increased with an increasing number of cigarettes smoked daily.

Multivariable-adjusted analyses showed that, compared with never-smokers, the relative risks of suicide were 1.2 for smokers of 10 or fewer cigarettes a day, 1.8 for smokers of 11-20 cigarettes a day, and 2.3 for smokers of more than 20 cigarettes a day. The relative risk of suicide for former smokers was 1.3. As in the general population, smokers in the cohort were more likely to have established risk factors for depression, such as being white, drinking heavily, not attending college and not exercising. After controlling for these factors, they found a strong, positive, and dose-related association between smoking and completed suicide. In other words, their findings indicated that the smoking-suicide connection was not explained by the greater tendency of smokers to be white, drink heavily, have less education, be of enlisted rank, and exercise less often. A limitation of this study was a lack information about some risk factors for suicide, including mental illness.

Smoking, Alcohol and Coffee: The "Everyday Substance Abuse Disorder"

Some authors have suggested that smoking cigarettes increases the risk of suicide if it is associated with heavy use of alcohol and coffee. Tanskanen et al. (2000) followed up 36,689 subjects in whom smoking was assessed using a standard set of questions. The amount of coffee drinking was determined with an open-ended question: "How many cups of coffee do you usually drink daily?" Alcohol intake was measured as the amount of pure alcohol used per week. In this sample, 138 suicides occurred among the men (55.0 per 100,000 per year) and 31 suicides among the women. The most common suicide methods were hanging (*n* =74), firearm (*n*= 39) and drug overdose (*n*=30). The results showed that the adjusted relative risk of suicide increased linearly with increasing level of joint heavy use of alcohol, cigarettes and coffee. According to the stress-diathesis model of the neurobiology of suicide (Mann, 1998), the authors suggested that alcohol and smoking are involved in serotonergic dysfunction, and caffeine can activate the noradrenaline neurons. Another hypothesis (Markou et al, 1998) suggests that people with mental health problems could self-medicate with alcohol, cigarettes and coffee in an attempt to obtain relief from the symptoms. However, in some circumstances, this self-medication may lead to substance abuse, which worsens the problem, eventually leading to suicidal behavior.

Iwasaki and coworkers (2005) examined a sample of 45,209 middle-aged Japanese men to investigate the following issues: (1) the effect of smoking status and the dose–response relationship, such as pack-years or number of cigarettes smoked per day; (2) the effect of smoking cessation; and (3) the effect of age at the start of smoking. The data came from from the Japan Public Health Center-based Prospective Study on Cancer and Cardiovascular Disease (JPHC Study), which began in 1990 for Cohort I and in 1993 for Cohort II. The study population was defined as all residents aged 40 to 59 years in Cohort I and 40 to 69 years in Cohort II. A self-administered questionnaire was distributed by hand or mail to the JPHC study subjects in 1990 (Cohort I) and in 1993 and 1994 (Cohort II). Among the eligible subjects, 45,452 men returned the questionnaire. The subjects were asked about their personal and family medical histories, anthropometric factors, smoking history, habitual intake of foods and beverages (including alcohol), physical activity, and other lifestyle factors. Questions concerning current or former smoking status, age at the start of smoking, number of cigarettes consumed per day, and age at the cessation of smoking were included in questionnaires. All registered subjects were followed from January 1 of the year of the baseline questionnaire survey until December 31, 1999 (Cohort I), and December 31, 2000 (Cohort II). During the follow-up period, 173 suicides occurred.

The results showed that current smokers with more than 60 pack-years of cigarettes had a significantly higher risk of suicide than that of never-smokers. Among current smokers, the suicide risk increased as the number of cigarettes smoked per day at baseline increased. This association was statistically significant even after adjusting for potential confounders such as the duration of smoking. The duration of smoking was not significantly associated with the suicide risk. The results indicated that heavy smokers, rather than long-term smokers, have a significantly increased risk of suicide. Additionally, since nicotine dependence has been associated with the risk of major depression (Breslau et al, 1993), the number of cigarettes smoked per day, rather than the duration of smoking, might be more strongly correlated with mental disorders, such as depression or one or more of the factors predisposing the subject to mental disorders that increase the risk of suicide (Harris & Barraclough, 1997). Another interesting result showed that the associations between subsequent suicide and the pack-years of cigarette smoking and the number of cigarettes smoked per day were somewhat attenuated, and the statistical significance disappeared, when the suicides which occurred during the first 2 years of the follow-up period were excluded. The statistical significance was preserved when subjects with a past history of chronic diseases were excluded. The lack of statistical significance might reflect the reduction in the number of cases or a lack of statistical power. Alternatively, the exclusion of the suicides that occurred during the first 2 years of the follow-up period, may have served as a control for the effects of mental illness on the risk of suicide to some extent.

Studies in the Psychiatric Population

Regarding mental health status, one study (Statham et al, 1998) investigated the clinical predictors of suicidal behavior after a major depressive episode in patients with a major depressive disorder or a bipolar disorder. The results supported a stress-diathesis model for suicidal behavior with stressors as precipitants for suicidal acts and a tendency toward pessimism and a propensity for aggression/impulsivity as the diathesis.

The authors studied a total of 308 patients, aged 18–75 years, with a DSM-III-R major mood disorder (79% with major depressive disorder and 21% with bipolar disorder) based on the Structured Clinical Interview for DSMIII-R (SCID). Exclusion criteria were current substance or alcohol abuse, neurological illness, or active medical conditions that could confound diagnosis and the clinical characterization of psychopathology. Patients were evaluated after 3 months, 1 year and 2 years. A multivariate Cox proportional hazards analysis, that included all correlates of past suicide attempts and additional risk factors identified from the literature, showed that a history of suicide attempt, a higher subjective rating of depression severity (using the Beck Depression Inventory), and cigarette smoking were the three strongest predictors. The effect of these predictors on the risk of suicidal acts in the follow-up period, was additive. In this study, smoking was associated with alcohol or other substance use disorder, and substance use disorders have been reported to increase the risk for eventual suicidal behavior (Statham et al, 1998).

This effect may be mediated through pharmacologically-induced disinhibition, depletion of monoamines, a common diathesis, or an association with relevant psychopathology such as aggression/ impulsivity. Perhaps some of the predictive power of cigarette smoking stems from its association with these other risk factors. Indeed, cigarette smokers have been found to have lower serotonergic functioning than nonsmokers (Malone et al, 2003) and more aggressive/impulsive traits (Meulemans et al, 1992; Tanskanen et al, 1998).

Iancu et al. (2006) studied the risk factors for suicidal behavior, using the suicide risk scale (SRS), in medicated smoking and medicated nonsmoking schizophrenic patients. In a small sample of 61 persons, they found a higher suicide risk in smoking patients and a trend for higher impulsivity. The small sample is a limitation of this study.

Recently Schneider and colleagues (2009) investigated the association between smoking and suicide among patients with personality disorders and affective disorders, with two hypotheses:

1 The association between psychiatric disorders, sociodemographic variables and suicide is modified by smoking status (never smokers, former smokers, and current smokers);
2 Adjustment for social factors and life events might alter the association between suicide, smoking status and psychiatric disorders.

In a sample of 263 suicides, the authors found that affective disorders predicted increased suicide risk in smokers, non-smokers, and former smokers, with the highest increased risk in never smokers. Suicide risk associated with substance use disorders was elevated by current smoking. No professional training and at least one significant life event during the last three months led to a higher increased suicide risk in smokers than in never and former smokers.

Three Longitudinal Studies

Breslau et al. (2005) studied a sample of 1,200 persons interviewed initially in 1989, with repeated assessments over a 10-year follow-up. The authors controlled for potential confounders, including major depression and substance abuse disorder. The results indicated an increased risk for subsequent suicidal thoughts or attempts associated with current daily smoking. A history of past daily smoking did not significantly predict subsequent suicidal thoughts or attempts.

The estimated risk for subsequent suicidal thoughts or attempts associated with current daily smoking was reduced somewhat when it was adjusted for major depression but remained significant. The estimated risk was further reduced when adjusted additionally for alcohol and drug use disorders but remained significant. The adjusted estimates of suicidal thoughts and attempts associated with current daily smoking were significantly higher than the estimates associated with past daily smoking. In other words, compared with never daily smokers, current daily smokers had an increased risk of subsequent suicidal thoughts or attempts. The limitations of the study were that there were no data on completed suicide and that the number of suicide attempts was small and was, therefore, combined with suicidal thoughts.

Kaisa et al. (2009) found that longitudinal smoking habits were a risk for early onset and repetitive suicide attempts in a cohort study of 12,058 persons. In this prospective longitudinal study, they found that the prevalence of hospital-treated suicide attempters was greater among prolonged smokers compared with ex-smokers and infrequent smokers in both sexes. During the follow-up period, up to the age of 39 years, female cohort members with prolonged or adult-onset smoking were found to be at increased risk for early-onset suicide attempts. Among men, a corresponding association was found only among adult smokers. A novel finding was that female cohort members with adult/prolonged smoking repeated suicidal acts more often than male cohort members.

Boden, Fergusson and Horwood (2007) found different results. In their 25-year longitudinal study, they found that the associations between the frequency of cigarette smoking and suicidal behavior may be explained largely by non-observed background factors and life circumstances that are associated with both cigarette smoking and suicidal behavior. In this study a birth cohort of 1,265 children (635 males, 630 females) born in the Christchurch (New Zealand) urban region in mid-1977 was studied at birth, 4 months, 1 year and annually to age 16, and again at ages 18, 21 and 25. The cohort was recruited by contacting all mothers giving birth in all Christchurch maternity hospitals during a 4-month period in mid-1977. The study has collected information from a variety of sources including parental interviews, teacher reports, self-reports, psychometric assessments, and medical and other records. The data were collected by trained interviewers via face-to-face or telephone interviews. A statistical analysis, conducted in three stages, has shown an evidence of clear and significant tendencies for increasing frequency of smoking to be associated with increasing levels of suicidal ideation and increasing rates of suicide attempts. After adjustment for fixed effects, there remained a modest, but statistically non-significant association between cigarette smoking and suicide attempts, suggesting that cigarette smoking does not play a causal role *per se* in increasing the risk of suicidal behavior and that these associations largely reflected the effects of non-observed background factors and adverse life experiences that are correlated with cigarette smoking and both suicidal ideation and suicide attempts.

b. Studies that Found an Indirect Relationship between Smoking and Suicide

Beratis et al. (1997) studied the positive association between smoking and suicide to see if this correlation could be secondary to existing psychological factors (see Doll & Peto, 1976). In this study, the authors started from the research that smokers have particular personality characteristics. For example, smokers have been described as more extraverted, (Eysenck et al, 1960) more psychopathic (McManus & Weeks, 1982) and more impulsive, with more risk-taking, danger-loving and belligerent behavior toward authority (Royal College of Physicians, 1977). In addition, smokers have been reported to be more disagreeable than nonsmokers (Smith, 1969), more spontaneous, more likely to seek stimuli, and more sensitive to feeling distressed. The sample was 100 consecutive suicide attempters admitted to a Greek General University Hospital from January 1992 to July 1995. Fifty-seven of these suicide attempters were female and 43 were male.

A semistructured interview was used to determine the residence, education, profession, marital status, previous suicidal behavior, psychopathology, tobacco smoking, age of initiation of smoking, and alcohol and illicit drug use. One hundred normal subjects matched for age, sex, socioeconomic and marital status, level of education, and place of residence (urban or rural) were used as controls. A second control group consisted of patients with psychiatric disorders matched with the suicide attempters for the parameters already mentioned and for the DSM-III-R diagnosis, age at onset, and approximate number of hospitalizations (designated psychiatric controls). The findings showed that those who smoke, particularly females and heavy smokers of both sexes, were at a greater risk for attempting suicide than those who did not smoke. This association might be either noncausal, resulting from the influence of factors predisposing to both smoking and suicidal behavior, or causal, resulting from a direct nicotine effect on brain function. Dysphoria, a pharmacological effect of nicotine ingested via smoking (Henningfield et al., 1985), could predispose susceptible individuals to impulsive behavior and suicide attempts. On the other hand, the observation that female suicide attempters had initiated smoking 3.3 years earlier than control subjects suggests that both cigarette smoking and suicide attempts are components of the same personality structure.

Kessler and coworkers (2008) studied the role of mental disorders in the consistently documented association between smoking and suicidal behavior. The data for the study derived from the National Comorbidity Survey Replication (NCS-R), a psychiatric epidemiological survey carried out in a multi-stage clustered area probability sample of the American household population between February 2001 and April 2003. The NCS-R interview was administered in two parts and included questions about suicidal behavior and smoking habits. DSM-IV psychiatric disorders were included as control variables in order to determine whether they statistically explained the association between smoking and suicidal behaviors. Both lifetime and past year disorders were assessed. All logistic regression analyses included controls for age, sex, race, ethnicity, marital status, employment status and family income, in order to control for the effects of ascribed status (i.e., age, sex, race-ethnicity), achieved status (i.e., marital status, employment status), and social statuses and socio-economic status (indicated by family income) that could be associated both with different norms regarding smoking and with differential risk for stressful experiences that predispose people to suicidal behaviors. The results demonstrated that statistically significant odds-ratios (2.9-3.1) were found between 12-month smoking and 12-month suicidal behaviors. However, the associations of smoking with the outcomes became nonsignificant after controls for DSM-IV psychiatric disorders. These findings are consistent with an interpretation that psychiatric disorders, or some causal factors of which psychiatric disorders are markers, cause both smoking and suicidal behaviors.

5. Smoking Cessation and Suicide Risk: Epidemiological Data

Smoking is an acknowledged to be an immense, increasing, modifiable risk factor for certain injuries, injury precursors and illnesses. Research indicates that smoking causes a physical dependence on nicotine, and this results in a withdrawal syndrome that includes worsened mood and other behaviors that would increase the risk of aggressive behavior and suicide attempts (Hughes, 2007a, 2007b). Many studies have found that negative affect symptoms are the most common symptoms of tobacco withdrawal, and several studies suggest that smoking cessation can precipitate a clinical depression in a subset of smokers (Hughes, 2006). Thus, increased suicidal behavior early after nicotine withdrawal is plausible. In contrast, most data indicate that prolonged abstinence for months or even years is associated with less, not more, depressed mood (US Department of Health and Human Services, 1990a).

Only one study has clearly quantified suicidal ideation early after smoking cessation. In this study, among 304 women who tried to stop smoking, 21 (7%) reported suicidal ideation during the 6 months post-cessation (Tsoh et al, 2000). Although this study lacked a control group, the rate of suicidal ideation is substantially elevated compared to epidemiological studies of smokers not trying to quit. A recent meta-analysis provided significant findings on whether cessation might change suicidal behavior (Leistikow & Shipley, 1999). This analysis searched for smoking cessation trials in which the rates of smoking cessation were ≥10% greater in the active versus the control condition and had a sufficient sample size to detect suicides. The study located three large randomized controlled trials in which the quit rates were 21%–24% greater in the active condition. The pooled rate of suicide in the control conditions in these studies was 0.22%. In the active conditions (in which much more smoking cessation occurred), it was 0.11%. This trend for fewer, not more, suicides in the group who had more abstinence was not statistically significant but certainly contradicts the hypothesis that cessation of smoking increases suicidal behaviors.

a. Association of Suicide and the Use of Smoking Cessation Medications

Two of the major medications for smoking cessation are full agonist nicotine replacement therapies (nicotine gum, patch, inhaler, lozenge/microtab and nasal spray) and the partial nicotine agonist varenicline (®Champix in England, French, Italy). Since full agonist nicotine replacement therapy (West & Shiffman, 2001) and partial agonist therapy (Fagerstrom & Hughes, 2008) both reduce nicotine withdrawal, including depression, this should reduce the appearance of suicidal behavior initially after cessation. On the other hand, since these medications are nicotine agents, the same arguments stated above – (a) nicotine is a psychological toxin and (b) since nicotine is an antidepressant, it might cause suicide – might apply. It could be argued that since varenicline is a partial agonist, its antidepressant effects should be less than that of full agonists and, therefore, the suicide risk should be less. On the other hand, varenicline does have antagonist effects, and nicotine antagonists appear to have antidepressant actions and, therefore, might have the potential to induce suicide (Rabenstein et al, 2006). Because of its potential effects on behavior, varenicline's influence on the mental functioning of the user should be considered in cases of suicide. Therefore, in cases of fatal outcome of patients under therapy with varenicline, a specific analysis for the drug should be performed.

There are two proven non-nicotine smoking cessation medications: antidepressants (McEwen et al, 2006; Hughes et al, 2007) and clonidine (Gourlay et al, 1999). The proven antidepressants are bupropion, an atypical antidepressant, and nortriptyline, a tricyclic antidepressant. The US Food and Drug Administration issued a warning that antidepressants could cause suicide (Gibbons et al, 2005). This warning was based on data from selective serotonin reuptake inhibitors (which are not effective for smoking cessation), but it has been extended to all antidepressants, including bupropion and nortriptyline (US Food and Drug Administration, 2007a). On the other hand, given that the biological or psychological mechanism of how antidepressants might increase the risk of suicide is unclear, it is unclear whether to expect an increased risk of suicide to occur also with nortriptyline and bupropion. Although there are no reports about suicide during the use of clonidine, an infrequent adverse event from clonidine is depressive symptoms which might lead to suicidal behavior. Rimonabant, a cannabinoid antagonist, is another nonnicotine medication being developed both as a treatment for obesity and for smoking cessation. In two post-mortem studies, completed suicides had higher levels of cannabinoid receptor activation than non-suicides (Vinod & Hungund, 2006). In addition, rimonabant acts similarly to SSRIs in its effects on neurotransmitters and in animal tests of antidepressant activity. Therefore, the antidepressant effects of rimonabant could cause it to increase suicidal behavior (Vinod & Hungund, 2006).

The main nicotine replacement therapies (NRT) are nicotine gum, inhaler, lozenge, microtab, nasal spray and patch (Fiore et al, 2008). Over 20,000 smokers have been exposed to full nicotine agonists via nicotine replacement therapy in published trials (Silagy et al, 2004). Meta-analyses and reviews of adverse events (AEs) from full nicotine agonists do not report increased suicidal behavior or worsened mood as plausible AEs from nicotine replacement (Silagy et al, 2004). The best test of the association of use of nicotine replacement and suicide comes from an analysis from the Lung Health Study, which randomly assigned smokers to nicotine gum or no medication. Over the 5 years of the study, the incidence of suicide was not greater in the nicotine gum versus the control group. If anything, suicides appeared to be less common in the nicotine gum group (0.05%) than in in the control group (0.25%). The only other data come from case reports of intentional overdoses of nicotine replacement therapy or bupropion. Interestingly, none of these attempts occurred in the context of using the medication to stop smoking. All appeared to be due to a pre-existing psychological or psychiatric problem.

b. Which Drug to be Used in Smoking Cessation?

From a review of recent literature, it could be recommended that the first agents to be used in smoking cessation treatment should be NRTs as they are the best documented product with mild side effects. It might be optimal to combine the patch with either gum, inhaler, sublingual tablets or nasal spray. In subjects that have failed with NRTs, varinicline should be the choice. Bupropion is preferred only for subjects with depression or smokers who have failed with the previous two agents, due to the many contra-indications and side effects of bupropion.

Nicotine vaccination is one promising new therapy under development that may have an effect on relapse. The principle is to induce nicotine antibodies into the blood so that inhaled nicotine from cigarette is prevented from reaching the CNS and, in that way, the pleasure from smoking is decreased.

6. Smoking and Suicide in Adolescence

Cigarette smoking among American adults has declined during the past 30 years but, among adolescents, smoking has increased more than 32% (National Center for Health Statistics, 1998). Daily smoking rates among high school seniors decreased between 1976 and 1984 from 28.8% to 18.7% but increased again to 24.6% by 1997 (Johnston, 1998). Despite public education about the dangers of tobacco use, adolescent smoking rates have decreased just slightly to 22.4% in 1998 from 24.6% reported in 1997 (Johnston, 1998). In 1998, the Centers for Disease Control and Prevention (CDC) reported current and frequent tobacco use among adolescents as risk behaviors that increased from 1991 to 1997 (CDC, 1998). Approximately 90% of adult smokers begin smoking as adolescents (Gorin & Arnold, 1998). The mean age of first-time use of tobacco is 14.5 years, and approximately 89% of daily smokers tried cigarettes by age 18 (Smith & Fiore, 1999). Data obtained from the 1997 Youth Risk Behavior Surveillance Survey (YRBSS) indicate that, of the 70.2% high school students who had tried cigarettes, 36.4% became current smokers and 16.7% became frequent smokers (CDC, 1998).

Suicidal behaviors have been associated with other problem behaviors that increase with age, including gun carrying, tobacco use, lack of seatbelt use, and condom nonuse (Brent et al, 1999; Brooks, Harris, Thrall, & Woods, 2002; Woods et al, 1997).The relative contribution of risk factors throughout the adolescent period, however, has yet to be examined thoroughly.

In the United States (Eaton et al, 2006), 71% of all deaths among youth and young adults aged 10-24 years result from four causes: motor vehicle crashes (31%), other unintentional injuries (14%), homicide (15%), and suicide (11%) (CDC, NCHS, 2006). Adolescent suicide and suicidal behaviors have caused great concern within the medical and public health community. Although the incidence of youth suicide has declined over the last decade, suicide remains one of the leading causes of adolescent mortality in the United States (Gould, Greenberg, Velting & Shaffer, 2003). While current annual rates for suicide are low (1.5 per 100,000 for 10–14 year olds and 8.2 per 100,000 for 15–19 year olds), rates of suicidal behaviors in community samples are much higher (De Man & Leduc, 1994; Lewinsohn, Rohde & Seeley, 1994; Reynolds, 1999). The 2001 Youth Risk Behavior Surveillance Survey (YRBS) conducted by the Centers for Disease Control and Prevention (CDC) found that 8.8% of youth had attempted suicide in the prior 12 months (CDC, 2003). Other epidemiological studies suggest that the lifetime rate of suicide attempts ranges from 3% to 15% (Lewinsohn, Rohde, Seeley & Baldwin, 2001).

Suicidal ideation is generally more common in young populations, suggesting important developmental issues (McAuliffe, 2002). In international comparisons of high school students, the prevalence of lifetime suicidal ideation was reported to vary from 19% to 44% (Tomori et al, 2001; Dervic et al, 2005; Liu, Tein, Zhao & Sandler, 2005; Miller & Taylor, 2005; Payci et al, 2005). The assessment of lifetime suicidal ideation is important because it may indicate tolerance of suicidal behavior as a potential coping option (McAuliffe, 2002). Indeed, it has been reported that attitudes exert a distal influence on behavior (Schuman & Johnson, 1976). For example, seeing suicide as a solution to problems might make an individual more prone to suicidal behavior in a crisis situation. Therefore, in addition to current suicidal thoughts, an individual's lifetime suicidal ideation should also be considered relevant in an assessment of suicide risk (McAuliffe, 2002).

Epidemiological studies indicate that the lifetime prevalence of suicide attempts among high school students ranges from 3% to 15% (Lewinsohn, Rohde, Seeley & Baldwin, (2001), with the rates being even higher among indigenous adolescents (up to 30%) (Kirmayer, Brass & Tait, 2000). Affective, disruptive, psychotic and substance abuse disorders are well-known risk predictors related to suicidal behavior in adolescence (Brent, 1995), and female gender is one of the strongest predictors of suicide ideation and attempts (Canetto & Sakinofsky, 1998).

Several explanations for the female predominance in nonfatal suicidal behavior exist and include lethality of methods, differential risk factors and differential socialization (Canetto & Sakinofsky, 1998). Among these, the differential risk factor explanation seems to be a valid potential explanation for the gender difference (Wichstrøm & Rossow, 2002). Adolescent females are found to be significantly more likely to report cigarette use in the past 30 days than are adolescent males (Aaron et al, 1995). Smoking among adolescent females has potential risks for their own future health and also for the infants born to adolescent mothers. Smoking during pregnancy has been implicated in small-for-gestational-age babies, perinatal loss, and premature rupture of membranes (American College of Obstetricians and Gynecologists, 1997). Adolescents engaging in risky behavior, such as drinking, smoking and/or sexual activity, are in increased odds for depression, suicidal ideation, and suicide attempts (Hallfors et al, 2004).

The influence of psychosocial risk factors on children's development and mental health is and has for a long time been a critical issue. Much effort has been made to identify risk factors as well as protective factors and to determine under which circumstances these factors operate (Rutter, 2000). Rohde et al. (2003), for example, included risk factors from 6 categories presumed to contribute to suicide-prone action, thoughts, and feelings for adolescents: demographic factors, suicide/depression, problem behavior factors, personality factors, parent/family factors, and peer factors. Beautrais (2000) noted that the risk factors related to youth suicidal behavior could be categorized into several domains including social and educational disadvantages, childhood and family adversity, psychopathology, individual and personal vulnerabilities, exposure to stressful life events and circumstances, and social, cultural, and contextual factors.

a. Predictors of Suicide in Adolescence

Adolescence has been conceptualized as a period in the lifespan characterized by numerous developmental challenges (e.g., identity formation and individuation from parents) and changes (e.g., puberty), and by the potential for high levels of associated stressful life events (Newcomb, Huba & Bentler, 1981; Windle, 1992). In this regard, research has consistently indicated higher levels of stressors among adolescent suicide attempters (de Wilde, Kienhorst, Diekstra & Wolters, 1992; Wilson et al, 1995) and completers (Brent, 1995) relative to nonsuicidal controls. Rickelman and Houfek (1995) reviewed research that indicated deficits in problem-solving abilities (e.g., dichotomous thinking and cognitive rigidity) among suicide attempters relative to nonsuicidal individuals. Kotila and Lonnqvist (1988) investigated the suicidal motives among a sample of 15-19 year-old hospitalized suicide attempters and found that an "escape or solution" motive was the one most frequently endorsed by the study's participants (by 35% of boys and 33% of girls). Psychological theories related to sex differences in coping styles and socialization processes offer explanations for these findings. Nolen-Hoeksema (1994) suggested that girls' coping styles are less action-oriented relative to boys' coping styles, and that adolescent girls are more likely to focus on and ruminate about their negative emotions than are boys. She further suggested that the interaction between a ruminative style of coping and higher levels of life stressors among girls accounts for their greater susceptibility to depression. Additionally, the gender intensification hypothesis (Hill & Lynch, 1983) suggests that the developmental period of adolescence is perceived by girls as a more stressful time due to socialization pressures, imposed by peers, parents and society, for girls to conform to traditional gender-specific behaviors (e.g., more interpersonal orientation, greater conformity and less achievement orientation). Whatever the mechanisms that account for sex differences during adolescence, research has been consistent in showing that adolescent girls experience higher levels of depressive symptoms, stressful life events, self-consciousness and social anxiety, and lower levels of self-esteem (Allgood-Merten, Lewinsohn, & Hops, 1990; Hill & Lynch, 1983).

Hemmingsson and Kriebel (2003) found that smoking at 18–20 years of age was associated with suicide during a follow-up period of 26 years. The trend of increasing suicide risk with increasing smoking that was observed is remarkably similar in magnitude to that reported for several other populations (Davey Smith, Phillips & Neaton, 1992; Miller, Hemenway & Rimm, 2000; Tanskanen et al, 2000; Leistikow, Martin & Samuels, 2000). However, unlike many previous studies, a number of indicators of mental well-being, substance abuse, and early life stresses were available for their analysis. When these factors were taken into consideration, there was little evidence for a smoking–suicide association among these young Swedish men. The increased risk of suicide among smokers in early adulthood was almost entirely explained by increased prevalence of people with low mental well-being and by substance abuse among smokers (Hemmingsson & Kriebel, 2003).

Smoking among youths is higher when parents, siblings, or peers smoke (Taylor et al, 2004; Johnson, Myers, Webber & Boris, 2004; Spijkerman, van den Eijnden, Vitale & Engels, 2004). Conduct disorder and parental smoking predicted earlier onset of daily cigarette smoking (Clark & Cornelius, 2004). In a survey of adolescent juvenile offenders, Helstrom et al. (2004) found that parental reports of externalizing problems were significantly related to self-reported tobacco use. Smoking is also higher in youths with histories of early conduct problems, drinking and illegal drug use, depression and suicidal behaviors. Among young people, early conduct problems and associated early onset of daily smoking predict a greater likelihood of becoming nicotine dependent.

Woods et al. (1997) studied 3,054 9th-12th grade adolescents to determine whether suicide attempts were associated with other risk and problem behaviors. Using stepwise logistic regression analysis, Woods found that significant predictors of attempted suicide by adolescents included (a) having had a physical fight (within the past 30 days), (b) regular cigarette use (within the past 30 days), (c) female gender, (d) alcohol (or other drug) use before the most recent sexual activity, (e) lifetime drug use, and (f) being Native

American or other races or ethnicities. (Other races and ethnicities were defined as those other than White, Black, Hispanic, and Asian.)

Early use of tobacco and early initiation of sexual intercourse are thought to be related. In a large study of 2,439 9th-12th grade public school students, the investigators found that the behavior most consistently associated with early initiation of sexual intercourse across all racial and gender groups included trying cigarettes and regular cigarette use before the age of 13 (Parillo, Felts & Mikow-Porto, 1997). Regular cigarette use before the age of 13 years was also significantly associated with early sexual intercourse initiation across all gender and racial groups except Black males.

Early cigarette initiation age often results in adult nicotine dependency (Chassin, Presson, Sherman & Edwards, 1990; Giovino et al, 1995). In a longitudinal study of 4,156 adults, researchers found a significant main effect of the school grade at which initiation of smoking occurred. The earlier the school grade of smoking onset, the greater risk of regular adult smoking (Chassin, Presson, Sherman, & Edwards, 1990) and an increase in smoking prevalence (tried cigarette smoking, used cigarettes frequently, and used cigarettes regularly) among students in higher grades (Kann et al, 1995). Parillo et al.'s (1997) research identified a relationship between cigarette smoking and early sexual initiation. According to the CDC (1994), the average age of first- time sexual experience is 17 years in females and 15 to 16 years in males.

Factors positively associated with a history of suicidal ideation are female gender, being a victim of bullying, lack of parental supervision, loneliness, age, current cigarette smoking, and alcohol use. Persistently high levels of problem drinking and depressive symptoms are associated with higher levels of suicidal thoughts and attempts. Higher levels of depressive symptoms and greater cigarette and illicit drug use distinguish suicidal ideators from attempters. Adolescents attempting suicide report lower levels of family social support, a greater use of substances to cope with stressors, and a higher density of substance-using peers (Windle & Windle, 1997). Moreover, Dong and colleagues (2005) found a graded relationship between the frequency of childhood residential moves and deleterious health outcomes throughout the lifespan, including early sexual initiation, teenage pregnancy, depressed affect, attempted suicide, smoking and alcoholism. Similarly, as the number of ACEs (Adverse Childhood Experiences) increased, the risk of these outcomes also increased. Thus, the apparent relationship between childhood residential mobility and negative health and social outcomes is mostly, if not solely, due to the effects of underlying ACEs that occur with high frequency in extremely mobile families. Children in these situations are likely coping with ACEs that have their own direct effects on childhood development and that may also exacerbate the vulnerabilities that accompany changes in residences, schools, and various social attachments.

All of these factors have been described as being associated with suicidal ideation in other studies (Lam et al, 2004; Borges, Walters & Kessler, 2000; McKeown et al, 1998; Parks, Schepp, Jang & Koo, 2006; Ali & Maharajh, 2005). It is also important to recognize that not all suicidal ideation will result in later suicide attempts or suicide (American Academy of Child and Adolescent Psychiatry Association, 2000). In line with the findings of previous longitudinal studies and reviews, a history of a suicidal act was found to be a significant predictor (Fergusson, Horwood, Ridder & Beautrais, 2005; Apter & King, 2006) irrespective of age, that is, it was a predictor across the entire period of adolescence (Lewinsohn, Rohde, Seeley & Baldwin, 2001; Lewinsohn, Rohde & Seeley, 1994; Fergusson, Beautrais & Horwood, 2003; Bridge, Goldstein & Brent, 2006; Foley, Goldston, Costello & Angold, 2006), while not living with both biological parents was a predictor relevant to middle adolescence (Wichstrøm, 2000) and a diagnosis of any depressive disorder was a predictor relevant to late adolescence/late adulthood (Lewinsohn, Rohde, Seeley & Baldwin, 2001; Bridge, Goldstein & Brent, 2006; Foley, Goldston, Costello & Angold, 2006), even when adjusted for familial, peer and individual factors. Nrugham and colleagues (2008) found that the quality of the relationship with parents and the use of stimulants, intoxicants and narcotics, although significant, differed according to age and the point in time in their importance as significant independent predictors of suicidal acts. Early indulgence in high risk behaviors such as use of alcohol or narcotics is significant in bivariate analyses (Lewinsohn, Rohde & Seeley, 1994), and daily smoking is significant as a bivariate predictor of suicidal acts performed up to early adulthood, indicating these as high risk factors across the entire period of adolescence.

In order to identify differences in risk factors for suicide attempts throughout adolescence, Hacker and colleagues (2006) conducted a school-based survey of ninth and eleventh graders. Suicide attempts were associated with cigarette and alcohol use, family violence, and depression for ninth graders and with illicit drug use, school violence, and sexual abuse for eleventh graders, while having friends was protective for both groups. Additionally, having more than one risk factor imparted an exponential risk for suicide attempts. There were important differences in the risk factors for ninth and eleventh graders consistent with the developmental changes of adolescence. "Worry about depression" was a predictor of suicide attempts for both groups. The risk of suicide attempts for ninth graders who were worried about depression was almost double that for eleventh graders. The relationship between depression and suicide attempts was not.

Lewinsohn et al. (2001) found that suicide attempts decreased with age more significantly than major depression did. While developmental maturation and decreasing impulsivity may be partly responsible for this change, it is also likely that psychopathology plays a more important role with age. This may be particularly true of substance abuse, which peaks in later adolescence. Brent et al.'s (1999) psychological autopsy study found that older adolescent suicides were more likely to be substance abusers and have conduct and mood disorders than younger suicides. Hacker and colleagues (2006) found that substance use increased the risk for suicide attempts for students in both grades. For ninth graders, alcohol and cigarette use made it into the final model, while for eleventh graders, other drugs played a more significant role.

The typical sequence of drug use in adolescence begins with cigarettes and alcohol and progresses to illicit substances (Kandel, Yamaguchi & Chen, 1992). While individual risk factors are significant predictors of suicide attempts, having multiple risk factors increases the risk for suicide attempts exponentially in both grades. The cumulative risk of exposure to violence, substance use and depression is of particular concern. Although true for both grades, this cumulative effect was particularly strong for ninth graders, suggesting that the impact of cumulative risk on younger adolescents may be greater. Risk behaviors are less frequent in ninth grade and their presence, therefore, is even more indicative of major problems. Identifying these students early and connecting them to services is an important step in prevention.

In another study based on students at the secondary grammar school Dervic et al. (2007) reported a comparatively greater prevalence of lifetime suicidal ideation and depression. In this context, a number of factors such as school stress, class, well-being, teacher support and grades/achievement have been reported to be associated with adolescent depression (Undheim & Sund, 2005) and suicidal ideation (De Man & Leduc, 1995). Given that school problems are a risk factor in youth suicidal behavior (Gould et al, 1996), the relationship between school-associated factors and adolescent suicidal ideation/behavior warrants further study in adolescents. Dervic et al. found that adolescent lifetime suicidal ideation was associated with substance problems and cigarette smoking. Substance problems are often reported as a risk factor in adolescent suicidal ideation and behavior (De Man & Leduc,

1995; Wu et al, 2004; Shaffer et al, 1996), and school pupils requiring the attention of health professionals for suicidal ideation or behavior should be asked about substance use and directed to appropriate treatment if necessary (Brener, Hassan & Barrios, 1999). Consistent with previous reports (King et al, 2001; Tomori et al, 2001; Takakura, Ueji & Sakihara, 2001; Hallfors et al, 2004), cigarette smoking was associated with suicidal ideation, even after adjusting for the presence of a mood disorder.

A study based on a community sample of urban high school students (Cho, Hallfors & Iritani, 2007) extended previous research by demonstrating that the association between onset of substance use and suicide risk indicators varies both by type of substance and by gender. Controlling for current substance use, it was found that, for boys, earlier initiation of hard drug use was significantly associated with all of the suicide risk factors, while early cigarette use was associated with suicide ideation. For girls, early onset of cigarette smoking was associated with suicide ideation, suicide ideation combined with alcohol and/or drug use, and endorsement of suicide. For girls, early onset of getting drunk was associated with depressive symptoms, and early onset of hard drug use was associated with suicide ideation combined with alcohol and/or drug use. Early onset of substance use is known to be a marker for co-occurring problem behaviors among adolescents. Thus, both early onset and current use of substances are related to suicide risk, and there are significant differences by gender as well as by type of substance use in these associations, especially in males. Males who are involved in behaviors such as smoking, drinking and using drugs, who are victims of bullying, and who have a homosexual orientation or bisexual orientation should be observed closely because they may have the potential for developing suicidal behavior (Parks, Schepp, Jang & Koo, 2006). Males who reported smoking were 2.6 times more likely to report suicidal ideation than males who did not report smoking. This may be related to the relationship of smoking and depression for males (Hurford, Smith & Cole, 2003; Weiss et al, 2005). Therefore, boys who have early onset of hard drug use should be screened for suicide risk and should be counseled to reduce or quit hard drug use. g Girls who had an early onset of smoking or alcohol use should similarly be screened.

Smoking is not only associated with suicide attempts, but also with self-mutilation behavior (Makikyro et al, 2004). However, the direction of the causality between smoking, attempted suicide, and self-mutilation remains unclear. Smoking adolescents who attempt suicide or mutilate themselves may have impaired catecholaminergic and 5-HT function in the CNS, leading to more impulsive and aggressive behavior than adolescents who have suicidal ideation alone (Linnoila & Virkkunen, 1992). Exposure to nicotine during adolescence causes changes in the CNS noradrenergic, dopaminergic, and serotonergic (5HT) function (Trauth et al, 2001; Xu et al, 2002). Thus, it is tempting to speculate that adolescents who smoke may be attempting to "self-medicate" their feelings of depression, despair, impulsivity and suicidality.

In conclusion, school health personnel and clinicians assessing suicidal risk among adolescents should be alerted to the importance of a history of a suicidal act, a diagnosis of any depressive disorder and not living with both biological parents as powerful potential predictors of suicidal acts from early adolescence to early adulthood.

b. Protective Factors

Protective factors for suicide in adolescence include family cohesion and stability, coping and problem solving skills, positive self-worth and impulse control, positive connections to school and extracurricular participation, academic success, good relationships with other youths, seeking adult help when needed, lack of access to suicidal means, access to mental health care, religiosity, and sports.

The protective role of youth involvement in sports and the lesser opportunity to smoke among youths involved in religious practice has also been reported. Chen and colleagues (2004) reported that the degree of religious practice is inversely related to the earliest stages of smoking (i.e., the first chance to try a cigarette and the first actual use). With increased religious practice, there was a reduced likelihood of smoking. The occurrence of the first actual use of tobacco was not associated with religious practice among youths who had already been exposed to the opportunity to try a cigarette. In a survey of Hungarian adolescents, Piko et al. (2004), reported that religiosity was inversely related to tobacco use. Those investigators also reported that membership of a sports club was inversely related to smoking.

c. Smoking, Suicide and Psychiatric Disorders in Adolescents

The association between smoking and suicidality has been studied among adult psychiatric patients (Mann et al, 1999; Tanskanen et al, 1998), but no previous studies have focused on adolescent psychiatric inpatients.

In a recent study (Riala, Viilo, Hakko & Rasanen, 2007), it was found that adolescents who are heavy daily smokers are at increased risk for suicidal attempts compared to non-smoking adolescents undergoing inpatient psychiatric hospitalization. This association was positive even after adjusting for the presence of psychiatric disorders. No association was observed between the heaviness of smoking and suicidal ideation. Among adolescents with severe psychiatric illnesses, heavy daily smoking may increase the risk of suicidal behavior independently of current psychiatric diagnosis. The degree of nicotine dependence of an adolescent should, therefore, be carefully assessed as part of a psychiatric evaluation.

Compared with current smokers, former smokers reported lower levels of delinquency, less coping through taking drugs, lesser availability of cigarettes, and less alcohol and marijuana use. Huebner and colleagues (2005) reported less depression, fewer suicidal thoughts, and fewer suicide attempts in former smokers than in current smokers. Makikyro et al. (2004), analyzed data from 157 patients (age 12–17 years) admitted to a psychiatric hospital in Oulu, Finland. They found that daily smoking was associated with suicide attempts after controlling for depression. In addition, adolescent smokers had three times greater risk for frequent self-mutilation. Hallfords et al. (2004), in a survey of 15–19-year-olds from the National Longitudinal Study of Adolescent Health, showed that smoking was associated with significantly increased odds of depression, suicidal ideation, and suicide attempts. The associations with suicidal ideation and attempt remained after statistical adjustment for depression. Toros et al. (2004) surveyed 4,256 Turkish adolescents (age 10–20 years) and found that regular smoking was associated with suicide attempts after controlling for depression.

As reported for both adults (Beratis, Lekka & Gabriel, 1997) and adolescents (Andrews et al, 2004; D'Eramo et al, 2004; Mäkikyrö et al, 2004), there is an increased frequency of psychiatric disorders among those who attempt suicide. Cigarette smoking has been reported to be more common among psychiatric patients with major depression (Hughes, Hatsukami, Michell & Dahlgren, 1986; Kendler et al, 1993), schizophrenia (Lohr & Flynn, 1992; Goff, Henderson & Amico , 1992; De Leon et al, 1995), and anxiety disorders (Breslau, Kilbey & Andreski, 1991; Glassman, 1993).

Smoking among adolescents with depressed mood or with a diagnosis of depression was not associated with a greater risk of suicidal ideation. Furthermore, despite reports to the contrary (Upadhyaya, Deas, Brady & Kruesi, 2002), tobacco smoking at age 15 was not predictive of later depressive disorder. A recent study (Fergusson, Goodwin & Horwood, 2003), suggested a small but significant association between depression and tobacco smoking and argued for a self-medication hypothesis whereby depressed individuals smoke to reduce their symptoms of depression. There are strong associations between anxiety and depression among young people (Fergusson, Goodwin & Horwood, 2003; McGee et al, 1990) and between smoking and anxiety disorders such as panic disorder (Breslau & Klein, 1999).

Previous studies have consistently reported that the prevalence of cigarette smoking among schizophrenic patients is higher than in the general population (Hughes, Hatsukami, Mitchell & Dahlgren, 1986; de Leon et al, 1995), a finding that has been interpreted as a reflection of self-medication for either symptoms of the disease or the adverse side effects of treatment. Weiser et al. (2004) reported that smokers were at higher risk for later onset of schizophrenia. Compared with nonsmokers, male adolescents who smoked one to nine cigarettes per day were 1.4 times more likely to be hospitalized for schizophrenia during the follow-up period, and adolescents who smoked 10 or more cigarettes per day were at 2.3 times greater risk. The latter difference remained statistically significant after controlling for cognitive performance, social adjustment, presence of non-psychotic mental illness, and socio-economic status. The authors noted the limitation due to the lack of data on use of cannabis (previously found to be associated with an elevated risk for schizophrenia) in this sample.

The significantly increased frequency of psychiatric disorders in the suicide attempters persisted after correction for several confounding factors including smoking (Menti et al, 2007). The independent effect of smoking on suicidal behavior from that caused by the presence of psychiatric disorders was also shown by the significantly greater frequency of smoking in the suicide attempters with psychiatric disorders than in non-suicidal control subjects matched for psychiatric disorder.

The significance of the smoking habits of adolescent psychiatric patients is often obscured by their severe other problems which may preclude attention to smoking. Smoking cessation should be supported because it may play a role in recovery from suicidality (Hintikka et al, 2001).

A surprisingly high proportion of the girls who smoked reported self-mutilation behavior. Suicidality among individuals with self-mutilation behaviors has often been underestimated and interpreted as manipulative or attention-seeking behavior. A recent study by Stanley et al. (2001) indicated that the number of suicide attempts or the lethality of the attempts did not differ between patients with and without a history of self-mutilation. Self-mutilators commonly underestimate the lethality of their suicidal behavior and view death with less finality. Depression, anxiety, disruptive disorders, and substance abuse/dependence have been found to be risk factors for attempted and completed suicides among teenagers (Gould et al, 1998; Marttunen et al, 1991; Shaffer et al, 1996). Many authors have noted that young women engage in more suicidal gestures, whereas young men have more completed suicides (Husain, 1990; King et al, 1993; Woods et al, 1997). Individuals with depression are also at a higher risk for attempting suicide and self-mutilation. According to some previous studies (King et al, 2002; Mann et al, 1999), smoking is independently associated with suicidality even after controlling for psychiatric diagnoses (Makikyro et al, 2004).

Two additional predictor variables have been found to contribute significantly to suicide attempts. These contributing factors exert an independent effect on suicidal behavior, including the effect of both smoking and presence of psychiatric disorders. Parent-child relational problems are by far the most frequent of the other conditions that may be a focus of clinical attention observed in slightly less than half of the attempted suicides, followed by relational problems. Of the psychosocial and environmental problems, health problems in family, parental overprotection, death of a family member, and parental divorce are the most frequent problems observed. It should be mentioned, however, that becoming drunk or any drinking, including alcohol and coffee, has been associated with suicidal ideation and suicide attempts (Hallfors et al, 2004; King et al, 2001). Other possible risk factors, such as the maternal and paternal smoking status does not contribute to attempting suicide. Hashish, a well-known risk factor (Breslau, Kilbey & Andreski, 1991; Glassman, 1993; Tomori et al, 2001) was the illicit substance used by only 3 attempters and 1 of the psychiatric control subjects. These findings indicate the relative importance of the risk factors that lead young people to make suicide attempts.

Menti et al. (2007), argued that the association between smoking and suicide attempts was related to personality characteristics of the smokers rather than to a direct effect of nicotine. Smokers are characterized by impulsivity, excitement seeking, low self-discipline, lack of careful consideration of the consequences of their actions, risk taking, thrill and danger seeking, emotional lability, rebelliousness, novelty seeking, and inattention (Tercyak & Audrain-McGovern, 2003; Terracciano & Costa, 2004; Dinn, Aycicegi & Harris, 2004; File, Dinnis, Heard & Irvine, 2002; Jacobs et al, 1966)

d. Children of Mothers at Psychosocial Risk

Life events of different types cause turmoil in the lives of children in a negative way. This exposure to negative life events may continue to affect the next generation.

Wadsby and colleagues (2007) showed that children, especially boys, of mothers who are exposed to psychosocial risks during pregnancy, particularly of those mothers with alcohol/drug problems, mental ill-health, poor self-image, negative life events and lack of confidence for their futures, reported more symptoms of poor mental health than children of non-risk mothers. It seems that there is a socially disadvantageous inheritance passed on from mothers at psychosocial risk to their children, and this affects the children and their functioning even when they have reached the age of 16. They have a more negative self-image, have experienced more life events of negative character that have been difficult to adjust to, and they more often have not successfully completed compulsory schooling. They have more often been placed in foster-care, are less satisfied with their school situation, and have a less positive opinion about their ability to direct their own future. Habitual smoking is more common among these teenagers. The girls in the index group more often had serious thoughts about committing suicide. In summary, this 16-year follow-up confirmed that children, especially boys, of psychosocial risk mothers are in many aspects worse off than children of non-risk mothers. In this respect, the outcome of the study was in line with the outcome of other longitudinal studies (Laucht et al, 2000a, 2000b, 2002), with the reservation that these later studies did not necessarily show differences related to gender.

e. Implications for Pediatric and Adolescent Nursing

School nurses, pediatric nurse practitioners, and others who work with adolescents should be aware of the interrelated nature of risk behaviors The identification of adolescents who are current smokers should alert health care providers to assess their clients for other problem behaviors. Early education, prevention, and intervention related to health risk behavior is essential in reducing levels of risk and should be initiated with school-aged and early adolescents in order to be effective in preventing negative outcomes. Other risky behaviors such as sexual activity, substance abuse, and fighting may prove more sensitive for adolescents than does smoking.

Parents and their children need education related to smoking and nicotine addiction beginning as early as elementary school. Parents should be aware that the early initiation of cigarette use increases the risk of addiction in later years and may be an indicator for other risk behaviors. School nurses have the potential for making an impact on the prevention of smoking among grade school children by educating parents about multiple-risk behaviors in early smokers.

f. Prevention

The continued high rates of suicide among adolescents (i.e., persons aged 15–19 years) and young adults (persons aged 20–24 years) have heightened the need for allocation of prevention resources. To better focus these resources, CDC's National Center for Injury Prevention and Control recently published *Youth Suicide Prevention Programs: A Resource Guide*. The guide describes the rationale and evidence for the effectiveness of various suicide prevention strategies and identifies model programs that incorporate these strategies. It is intended as an aid for communities interested in developing or augmenting suicide prevention programs targeted toward adolescents and young adults. There are eight prevention strategies described in the Resource Guide.

School gatekeeper training. This type of program is designed to help school staff (e.g., teachers, counselors, and coaches) identify and refer students at risk for suicide. These programs also teach staff how to respond to suicide or other crises in the school.

Community gatekeeper training. These programs train community members (e.g., clergy, police, merchants, and recreation staff) and clinical health-care providers who see adolescent and young adult patients (e.g., physicians and nurses) to identify and refer persons in this age group who are at risk for suicide.

General suicide education. Students learn about suicide, its warning signs, and how to seek help for themselves or others. These programs often incorporate a variety of activities that develop self-esteem and social competency.

Screening programs. A questionnaire or other screening instrument is used to identify high-risk adolescents and young adults and provide further assessment and treatment. Repeated assessment can be used to measure changes in attitudes or behaviors over time, to test the effectiveness of a prevention strategy, and to detect potential suicidal behavior.

Peer support programs. These programs, which can be conducted in or outside of school, are designed to foster peer relationships and competency in social skills among high-risk adolescents and young adults.

Crisis centers and hotlines. Trained volunteers and paid staff provide telephone counseling and other services for suicidal persons. Such programs also may offer a "drop-in" crisis center and referral to mental health services.

Restriction of access to lethal means. Activities are designed to restrict access to handguns, drugs, and other common means of suicide.

Intervention after a suicide. These programs focus on friends and relatives of persons who have committed suicide. They are designed to help prevent or contain suicide clusters and to help adolescents and young adults cope effectively with the feelings of loss that follow the sudden death or suicide of a peer.

Integrated prevention strategies that address multiple associated factors (e.g., substance abuse prevention, family and peer support, and access to health services) are likely to be more effective in reducing suicidal behavior than programs that focus on a single risk factor (Anderson et al, 2001).

7. Conclusions

Despite the large literature available about smoking as direct risk factor for suicide, the findings are not yet consistent. It is clear that the prevalence of smoking is higher in suicidal people, but it is less certain that smoking itself (or the nicotine effect on brain function) is directly involved in suicidality. Other elements associated with both suicide and smoking may be implicated in this relationship. Inclusion of data on important confounds (i.e., the presence of debilitating smoking-related illness, psychiatric disorder, withdrawal symptoms and patterns of medication use) is necessary. Most likely, several factors contribute to an increased rate of suicidal behavior in current smokers. The three most plausible (but relatively untested) explanations for the association are (1) that smokers have preexisting conditions that increase their risk for suicide, (2) smoking causes painful and debilitating conditions that might lead to suicide, and (3) smoking decreases serotonin and monoamine oxidase levels. Stopping smoking appears to lead to major depression in some smokers and, therefore, it could induce suicide. However, smoking cessation has not been associated with suicide in the few studies conducted. Regulatory agencies have stated that bupropion, rimonabant and varenicline appear to be associated with suicide, but the data for these statements have not been presented in sufficient detail to assess their validity.

The present review indicates that there are important gender differences in the association between substance use and suicide risk. The review also underscores the importance of preventing the early onset of substance use to alleviate mental health problems related to suicide.

Further research is needed to explore the causal mechanisms of gender-specific substance use behavior and suicide risk factors. As Fergusson and Lynskey (1995) suggested, the value of identifying variables that successfully distinguish suicide attempters from ideators relates to our increased ability to identify those adolescents who are at greatest risk for attempting suicide based on their "burden" of psychosocial and behavioral risk indicators.

REFERENCES

Aaron D. J., Dearwater, S. R., Anderson, R., et al (1995). Physical activity and the initiation of high-risk health behaviors in adolescents. *Official Journal of the American College of Sports Medicine, 27 (12)*: 1639-1645.

Adler, L. E., Olincy, A., Waldo, M., et al. (1998). Schizophrenia, sensory gating, and nicotinic receptors. *Schizophr Bull, 24 (2)*: 189-202.

Ali, A. & Maharajh, H. D. (2005). Social predictors of suicidal behaviour in Trinidad and Tobago. *Soc Psychiatry Psychiatric Epidemiol 40*, 186-91.

Allgood-Merten, B., Lewinsohn, P. M. & Hops, H. (1990). Sex differences and adolescent depression. *Journal of Abnormal Psychology*, *99*, 55-63.

American Academy of Child and Adolescent Psychiatry Association, (2000). Practice Parameters for the assessment and treatment of children and adolescents with suicidal behaviours. [http://www.aacap.org/galleries/PracticeParameters/Suicide.pdf].

American College of Obstetricians and Gynecologists, (1997). Smoking and women's health. *ACOG Educational Bulletin. No. 240*. Washington, DC: Author.

American Psychiatric Association (APA), (2000). Diagnostic and statistical manual for mental disorders 4th edition, *Text Revision. Washington, DC: Author.*

Anderson, R. N., Minino, A. M., Fingerhut, L. A., et al. (2001). *Natl Vital Stat Rep*, *52*, 1–5.

Andrews, J. A. & Lewinsohn, P. M. (1992). Suicidal attempts among older adolescents: prevalence and co-occurrence with psychiatric disorders. *J Am Acad Child Adolesc Psychiatry 31*, 655-62.

Angst, J. & Clayton, P. J. (1998). Personality, smoking and suicide: a prospective study. *J Affect Disord, 51 (1)*, 55-62.

Apter, A. & King, R. A. (2006). Management of the depressed suicidal child or adolescent. *Child Adolesc Psychiatr Clin N Am 15 (4)*, 999–1013.

Audrain-McGovern, J., Lerman, C., Wileyto., E. P., et al. (2004). Interacting effects of genetic predisposition and depression on adolescent smoking progression. *Am J Psychiatry*, *161*, 1224–1230.

Balfour, D. J. & Ridley, D. L. (2000). The effects of nicotine on neural pathways implicated in depression: a factor in nicotine addiction? *Pharmacol Biochem Behav*, *66 (1*), 79-85.

Beautrais, A. L. (2000). Risk factors for suicide and attempted suicide among young people. *Aust N Z J Psychiatry*, *34*, 420–436.

Benwell, M., Balfour, D & Anderson, J. (1990). Smoking-associated changes in the serotonergic systems of discrete regions of human brain. *Psychopharmacology 102*, 68-72.

Beratis, S., Lekka., N. P. & Gabriel, J. (1997). Smoking among suicide attempters. *Compr Psychiatry*, *38*, 74-9.

Berlin, I., Said, S., Spreux-Varoquaux, O., et al. (1995). Monoamine oxidase A and B activities in heavy smokers. *Biol Psychiatry 38*, 756-761.

Bernal, M., Haro, J. M., Bernert, S., et al, the ESEMED/MHEDEA Investigators, (2007) Risk factors for suicidality in Europe: results from the ESEMED study. *J Affect Dis*, *101*, 27–34.

Boden, J. M., Fergusson, D. M. & Horwood, L. J. (2008). Cigarette smoking and suicidal behaviour: results from a 25-year longitudinal study. *Psychological Medicine*, *38*, 433–439.

Borges, G., Walters, E. E. & Kessler, R. C. (2000). Associations of substance use, abuse, and dependence with subsequent suicidal behavior. *Am J Epidemiol, 151*, 781-9.

Brener, N. D., Hassan, S. S. & Barrios, L. C. (1999). Suicidal ideation among college students in the United States. *J Consult Clin Psychol 67*, 1004–1008.

Brent, D. A., (1995). Risk factors for adolescent suicide and suicidal behaviour: Mental and substance abuse disorders, family environmental factors, and life stress. *Suicide and Life Threatening Behaviour 25*, 52–63.

Brent, D. A., Baugher, M., Bridge, J., et al, (1999). Age- and sex-related risk factors for adolescent suicide. *Journal of the American Academy of Child and Adolescent Psychiatry 38*, 1497–1505.

Breslau, N., Kilbey, M. M. & Andreski, P. (1991). Nicotine dependence, major depression, and anxiety in young adults. *Arch Gen Psychiatry*, *8*, 1069-74.

Breslau, N., Kilbey, M. M. & Andreski, P. (1993). Nicotine dependence and major depression. New evidence from a prospective investigation. *Arch Gen Psychiatry*, *50 (1)*, 31-5.

Breslau, N., Fenn, N. & Peterson, E. L. (1993c). Early smoking initiation and nicotine dependence in a cohort of young adults. *Drug Alcohol Depend 33*, 129–37.

Breslau, N; Peterson, E. L., Schultz, L. R., et al. (1998). Major depression and stages of smoking. A longitudinal investigation. *Arch Gen Psychiatry*, *55 (2)*, 161-6.

Breslau, N. & Klein, D. F. (1999). Smoking and panic attacks: an epidemiologic investigation. *Arch Gen Psychiatry*, *56*, 1141–1147.

Breslau, N., Johnson, E. O., Hiripi, E. & Kessler, R. (2001). Nicotine dependence in the United States: prevalence, trends, and smoking persistence. *Arch Gen Psychiatry*, *58 (9)*, 810–816.

Breslau, N., Novak, P. & Kessler., R. C., (2004). Daily smoking and the subsequent onset of psychiatric disorder. *Psychol Med*, *34*, 323–33.

Breslau, N., Schultz, L. R., Johnson, E. O., et al. (2005). Smoking and the risk of suicidal behavior: a prospective study of a community sample. *Arch Gen Psychiatry*, *62*, 328-334.

Bridge, J. A., Goldstein, T. R. & Brent, D. A. (2006). Adolescent suicide and suicidal behaviour. *J Child Psychol Psychiatry*, *47 (3/4)*, 372–394.

Brooks, T. L., Harris, S. K., Thrall, J. S. & Woods, E. R., (2002). Association of adolescent risk behaviors with mental health symptoms in high school students. *Journal of Adolescent Health*, *31*, 240–246.

Brown, R. A., Lewinsohn, P. M., Seeley, J. R. & Wagner, E. F. (1996). Cigarette smoking, major depression, and other psychiatric disorders among adolescents. *J Am Acad Child Adolesc Psychiatry 35 (12),* 1602-10.

Canetto, S. S. & Sakinofsky, I. (1998). The gender paradox in suicide. *Suicide and Life Threatening Behaviour*, *28 (1*), 1–23.

Casey, P. R., Dunn, G., Kelly, B. D., et al. on behalf of the ODIN group, (2006). Factors associated with suicidal ideation in the general population. Five-centre analysis from the ODIN study. Br J Psychiatry 189, 410–415.

CDC, (1992) . Youth suicide prevention programs: a resource guide. *Atlanta: US Department of Health and Human Services, Public Health Service*

CDC, (2008). Annual smoking-attributable mortality. Cigarette Smoking Among Adults-United States. *Morbidity and Mortality Weekly Report (MMWRs) (45)*, 1226–1228.

CDC, NCHS, (2006). Public Use Data File and Documentation: Multiple Cause of Death for ICD-10 2003 Data. [book on CD-ROM]. *Hyattsville, Md: National Center of Health Statistics*

Centers for Disease Control & Prevention, (1994). Medical care expenditures attributable to cigarette smoking—United States, 1993. *Morbidity and Mortality Weekly Report*, *43 (26)*, 469-472.

Centers for Disease Control and Prevention, (2008). Targeting Tobacco Use: The Nation's Leading Cause of Preventable Death

Chassin, L., Presson, C. C., Sherman, S. J. & Edwards, D. A. (1990). The natural history of cigarette smoking: Predicting young-adult smoking outcomes from adolescent smoking patterns. *Health Psychology*, *9 (6)*, 701-716.

Chen, C. Y., Dormitzer, C. M., Bejarano, J. & Anthony, J. C. (2004). Religiosity and the earliest stages of adolescent drug involvement in seven countries of Latin America. *Am J Epidemiol 159*, 1180–1188.

Chen, C. Y., Dormitzer, C. M., Gutierrez, U., et al. (2004). The adolescent behavioural repertoire as a context for drug exposure: behavioral autarcesis at play. *Addiction, 99*, 897–906.

Cherpitel, C. J., Borges, G. L. & Wilcox, H. C. (2004). Acute Alcohol Use and Suicidal Behavior: A Review of the Literature. *Alcohol Clin Exp Res*, *28 (5),* 18S-28S.

Chiles, J. A., Benjamin, G. A. & Cahn T. S. (1990). Who smokes? Why? Psychiatric aspects of continued cigarette usage among lawyers in Washington State. *Compr Psychiatry*, *31*, 176-18.

Cho, H., Hallfors, D. D. & Iritani, B. J., 2007. Early initiation of substance use and subsequent risk factors related to suicide among urban and high school students. *Addict Behav 32*, 1628–1639.

Choi, W. S., Patten, C. A., Gillin, J. C., 6 et al, (1997). Cigarette smoking predicts development of depressive symptoms among U.S. adolescents. *Ann Behav Med, 19 (1),* 42-50.

Clark, D. B. & Cornelius, J. (2004). Childhood psychopathology and adolescent cigarette smoking: a prospective survival analysis in children at high risk for substance use disorders. *Addict Behav*, *29*, 837–841.

Covey, L. S., Glassman, A. H. & Stetner, F. (1997). Major depression following smoking cessation. *Am J Psychiatry*, *154 (2)*, 263-5.

Dalack, G. W., Healy, D. J. & Meador-Woodruff, J. H. (1998). Nicotine dependence in schizophrenia: clinical phenomena and laboratory findings. *Am J Psychiat 155*, 1490-1501.

Davey Smith, G., Phillips, A. N. & Neaton, J. D. (1992). Smoking as 'independent' risk factor for suicide: illustration of an artifact from observational epidemiology? *Lancet*, *340*, 709–12.

de Leon, J. & Diaz, F. J. (2005). A meta-analysis of worldwide studies demonstrates an association between schizophrenia and tobacco smoking behaviors. *Schizophr Res*, *76 (2-3)*, 135-57.

De Leon, J., Canuso, C., White, A. O., et al. (1995). Schizophrenia and smoking: an epidemiological survey in a state hospital. *Am J Psychiatry*, *152*, 453-455.

De Leon, J., Rendon, D. M., Baca-Garcia, E., et al, (2007). Association between smoking and alcohol use in the general population: stable and unstable odds ratios across two years in two different countries. *Alcohol Alcohol*, *42 (3),* 252-7.

De Man, A. F. & Leduc, C. P., (1994). Validity and reliability of a self-report suicide ideation scale for use with adolescents. *Social Behavior and Personality*, *22*, 261–266.

De Man, A. F. & Leduc, C. P. (1995). Suicidal ideation in high school students: depression and other correlates. *J Clinical Psychology*, *51*, 173–181.

De Wilde, EJ, Kienhorst, 1CWM, Diekstra, RFW & Wolters, WHG, (1992). The relationship between adolescent suicidal behavior and life events in childhood and adolescence. *American Journal of Psychiatry 149*, 45-51.

Degenhardt, L. & Hall, W. (2001). The relationship between tobacco use, substance-use disorders and mental health: results from the National Survey of Mental Health and Well-being. *Nicotine Tob Res 3 (3)*, 225-34.

'Eramo, D., Prinstein, K. S., Freeman, M. J., et al. (2004). Psychiatric diagnoses and comorbidity in relation to suicidal behavior among psychiatrically hospitalized adolescents. *Child Psychiatry Hum Dev*, *35*, 21-35.

Dervic, K., Akkaya-Kalayci, T., Kapusta, N. D., et al. (2007). Suicidal ideation among Viennese high school students. *Wien Klin Wochenschr 119 (5-6)*, 174-80.

Dervic, K., Csorba, J., Rosza, S., et al, (2005). Attitudes towards suicide and help-seeking in Hungarian adolescents. *J Am Acad Child Adolesc Psychiatry 44*, 628–629.

Dinn, W. M., Aycicegi, A. & Harris, C. L. (2004). Cigarette smoking in a student sample: neurocognitive and clinical correlates. *Addict Behav*, *29*, 107-26.

Doll, R. & Peto, R. (1976). Mortality in relation to smoking: 20 years' observations on male British doctors. *Br Med J 2*, 1525-1536.

Dong, M., Anda, R. F., Felitti, V. J., et al, (2005). Childhood residential mobility and multiple health risks during adolescence and adulthood: the hidden role of adverse childhood experiences. *Arch Pediatr Adolesc Med 159 (12)*, 1104-10.

Eaton, D. K., Kann, L., Kinchen, S., et al, (2006). Youth risk behavior surveillance--United States, 2005. *J Sch Health, 76 (7)*, 353-72.

Ellis, T. E. & Trumpower, D. (2008). Health-risk behaviors and suicidal ideation: a preliminary study of cognitive and developmental factors. *Suicide Life Threat Behav*, *38 (3),* 251-9.

Eysenck, H. J., Tarrant, M., Woolf, M. & England, L. (1960). Smoking and personality. *Br Med J 1*, 1456-1460.

Fagerstrom, K. & Hughes, J. R. (2008). Integrating varenicline into the treatment of tobacco dependence. *Neuropsychiatr Dis Treat*, *4*, 1–11

FDA alert 7/2005. Bupropion hydrochloride (marketed as the antidepressant Wellbutrin) Information http://www.fda.gov/cder/drug/*infopage/ bupropion/default.htm*

FDA05/16/2008. Public Health Advisory Important Information on Chantix (varenicline) *http://www.fda.gov/cder/drug/advisory/varenicline.htm*

Fergusson, D. M. & Lynskey, M. T. (1995). Suicide attempts and suicidal ideation in a birth cohort of 16-year-old New Zealanders. *Journal of the American Academy of Child and Adolescent Psychiatry* , *34*, 1308-1317.

Fergusson, D. M., Beautrais, A. L. & Horwood, L. J. (2003). Vulnerability and resiliency to suicidal behaviours in young people. *Psychol Med*, *33*, 61–73.

Fergusson, D. M., Goodwin, R. D. & Horwood, L. J. (2003). Major depression and cigarette smoking: results of a 21-year longitudinal study. *Psychol Med*, *33*, 1357–1367.

Fergusson, D. M., Horwood, L. J., Ridder, E. M. & Beautrais, A. (2005). Suicidal behaviour in adolescence and subsequent mental health outcomes in young adulthood. *Psychol Med*, *35*, 983–993.

File, S. E., Dinnis, A. K., Heard, J. E. & Irvine, E. E. (2002). Mood differences between male and female light smokers and nonsmokers. *Pharmacol Biochem Behav*, *72*, 681-9.

Fiore, M., Jaen, C., Baker, T., et al. (2008). Treating Tobacco Use and Dependence: Clinical Practice Guideline. US Public Health and Human Services, Washington, DC.

Foley, D. L., Goldston, D. B., Costello, E. J. & Angold, A. (2006). Proximal psychiatric risk factors for suicidality in youth. The Great Smoky Mountains Study. *Arch Gen Psychiatry*, *63*, 1017–1024.

Fotti, S. A., Katz., L. Y., Afifi, T. O. & Cox, B. J. (2006). The associations between peer and parental relationships and suicidal behaviours in early adolescents. *Can J Psychiatry*, *51 (11)*, 698–703.

Fowler. J. S., Logan, J., Wang, G. J. & Volkow, N. D. (2003). Monoamine oxidase and cigarette smoking. *Neuro Toxicology*, *24*, 75–82.

Gibbons, R., Hur, K., Bhaumik, D. & Mann, J. (2005). The relationship between antidepressant medication use and rate of suicide. *Arch Gen Psychiatr*, 62, 165–172.

Giovino, G. A., Henningfield, J. E., Tomar, S. L., et al. (1995). Epidemiology of tobacco use and dependence. *Epidemiologic Reviews 17 (1)*, 48-65.

Glassman, A. H., (1993). Cigarette smoking: implications for psychiatric illness. *Am J Psychiatry*, *150*, 546-53.

Glassman. A. H., (1988). Heavy smokers, smoking cessation and clonidine. *Journal of the American Medical Association (JAMA)*, *259*, 2863-2866.

Glassman, A. H., Helzer. J. E., Covey, L. S., et al, (1990). Smoking, smoking cessation and major depression. *JAMA, J Am Med Assoc*, *264*, 1549–1564.

Goff, D. C., Henderson, D. C. & Amico, E. (1992). Cigarette smoking in schizophrenia: relationship to psychopathology and medication side effects. *Am J Psychiatry*, *149*, 1189-94.

Goodman, E. & Capitman, J. (2000). Depressive symptoms and cigarette smoking among teens. *Pediatrics*, *106*, 748-755.

Gorin, S. & Arnold, J. (1998). Health promotion handbook. *St. Louis: Mosby, Inc.*

Gould, M., King, R., Greenwald, S., et al. (1998). Psychopathology associated with suicidal ideation and attempts among children

Gould, M. S., Fisher, P., Parides, M., et al. (1996). Psychosocial risk factors of child and adolescent completed suicide. *Arch Gen Psychiatry 53*, 1155–1162.

Gould, M. S., Greenberg, T., Velting, D. M. & Shaffer, D. (2003). Youth suicide risk and preventive intervention: A review of the past 10 years. *Journal of the American Academy of Child and Adolescent Psychiatry 42*, 386–405.

Gourlay, S. G., Stead, L. F. & Benowitz, N. L., (1999). Clonidine for smoking cessation. The Cochrane Library, www.thecochranelibrary.com.

Grant, B. F., Hasin, D. S., Coun, S. P., et al. (2004). Nicotine dependence and psychiatric disorders in the United States: results from the national epidemiologic survey on alcohol and related conditions. *Archives of General Psychiatry*, *61*, 1107–1115.

Hacker, K. A., Suglia, S. F., Fried, L. E., et al. (2006). Developmental differences in risk factors for suicide attempts between ninth and eleventh graders. *Suicide Life Threat Behav*, *36 (2)*, 154-66.

Hallfors, D. D., Waller, M. W., Ford, C. A., et al. (2004). Adolescent depression and suicide risk: association with sex and drug behavior. *Am J Prev Med*, *27*, 224–231.

Harris, E. C. & Barraclough, B. (1997). Suicide as an outcome for mental disorders. A meta-analysis. *Br J Psychiatry 170*, 205–228.

Harrison, E. L. Desai, R. A. & McKee, S. A., (2008). Nondaily smoking and alcohol use, hazardous drinking, and alcohol diagnoses amongyoung adults: findings from the NESARC. *Alcohol Clin Exp Res*, *32 (12),* 2081-7.

Heatherton, T. F., Kozlowski, L. T., Frecker, R. C., et al. (1989). Measuring the heaviness of smoking: using self-reported time to the first cigarette of the day and number of cigarettes smoked per day. *Br J Addict*, *84*, 791-800.

Helstrom, A., Bryan, A., Hutchison, K. E., et al. (2004). Tobacco and alcohol use as an explanation for the association between externalizing behavior and illicit drug use among delinquent adolescents. *Prev Sci 5*, 267–277.

Hemenway, D., Solnick, S. J. & Colditz, G. A. (1993). Smoking and suicide among nurses. *Am J Public Health*, *83 (2)*, 249-51.

Hemmingsson, T. & Kriebel, D. (2003). Smoking at age 18-20 and suicide during 26 years of follow-up-how can the association be explained? *Int J Epidemiol*, *32 (6*), 1000-4.

Henningfield, J. E., Miyasato, K. & Jasinski, D. R. (1985). Abuse liability and pharmacodynamic characteristics of intravenous and inhaled nicotine. *J Pharmacol Exp Ther 234*, 1-12.

Hill, J. P. & Lynch, M. E. (1983). The intensification of gender related role expectations during early adolescence. In J: Brooks-Gunn & A. C. Petersen (Eds.), Girls at puberty: *Biological and psychosocial perspectives* (pp. 201-228). New York: Plenum Press

Hintikka, J, Pesonen, T, Saarinen, P & et al, (2001). Suicidal ideation in the Finnish general population. A 12-month follow-up study. *Soc Psychiatry Psychiatr Epidemiol 36*, 590 –4.

Hintikka, J., Koivumaa-Honkanen, H., Lehto, S. M., et al. (2009). Are factors associated with suicidal ideation true risk factors? : A 3-year prospective follow-up study in a general population. *Soc Psychiatry Psychiatr Epidemiol 44 (1)*, 29-33.

Horesh, N., Rolnick T., Iancu, I., et al. (1997). Anger, impulsivity and suicide risk. *Psychother Psychosom*, *66 (2)*, 92-96.

Huebner, A. J., Shettler, L., Matheson, J. L., et al. (2005). Factors associated with former smokers among female adolescents in rural Virginia. *Addict Behav*, *30*, 167–173.

Hughes, J. R., Hatsukami, D. K., Michell, J. E., & Dahlgren L. A. (1986). Prevalence of smoking among psychiatric outpatients. *Am J Psychiatry*, *143*, 993-7.

Hughes, J. R. (2006). Depression during tobacco abstinence. *Nicotine Tobacco Res*, *9*, 443–446.

Hughes, J. R. (2007a). The effects of abstinence from tobacco: etiology, determinants, epidemiology, significance. *Nicotine Tobacco Res*, *9*, 329–339.

Hughes, J. R., (2007b). The effects of abstinence from tobacco: valid symptoms and time course. *Nicotine Tobacco Res, 9*, 315–327.

Hurford, D. P., Smith, J. V. & Cole A. (2003). The relationship between depression and smoking in adolescents. *Adolescence*, *38*, 149-157.

Husain, S. A. (1990). Current perspective on the role of psychological factors in adolescent suicide. *Psychiatr Ann*, *32*, 122–7.

Iancu, I., Sapir, A. P. & Shaked, G. (2006). Increased suicidal risk among smoking schizophrenia patients. *Clin Neuropharmacol.*, *29 (4)*, 230-7.

Istavan, J. & Matarazzo, J. (1984). Tobacco, alcohol and caffeine use: a review of their interrelationships. *Psychol Bull, 16*, 244-273.

Iwasaki, M., Akechi, T., Uchitomi, Y. & Tsugane, S. (2005). Cigarette smoking and completed suicide among middle-aged men: a population-based cohort study in Japan. *Ann Epidemiol, 15 (4)*, 286-92.

Jacobs, M. A., Anderson, L. S., Champagne, E., et al, (1966). Orality, impulsivity, and cigarette smoking in men: further findings in support of a theory. *J Nerv Ment Dis 143*, 207-19.

John, U., Meyer, C., Rumpf, H. J. Hapke, U. (2003). Probabilities of alcohol high-risk drinking, abuse or dependence estimated on grounds of tobacco smoking and nicotine dependence. *Addiction, 98 (6),* 805-14.

Johnson, C. C., Myers, L., Webber, L. S. & Boris, N. W. (2004). Profiles of the adolescent smoker: models of tobacco use among 9th grade high school students; Acadiana Coalition of Teens against Tobacco (ACTT). *Prev Med, 39*, 551–558.

Johnston, L. D. (1998). National survey results on drug use from the monitoring the future study: 1975-1997: Secondary School Students. *Washington, DC: US Government Printing Office*

.Kamali, M., Oquendo, M. A. & Mann, J. J. (2001). Understanding the neurobiology of suicidal behavior. *Depress Anxiety, 14 (3)*, 164-76.

Kandel, D. B., Yamaguchi, K. & Chen, K. (1992). Stages of progression in drug involvement from adolescence to adulthood: Further evidence for the gateway theory. *Journal of Studies in Alcohol, 53*, 446–457.

Kann, L., Warren, C. W., Harris, W. A., et al. (1995). Youth risk behavior surveillance–United States, 1993. *Journal of School Health, 65 (5)*, 163-170.

Kassel, J. D. (1997). Smoking and attention: a review and reformulation of the stimulus-filter hypothesis. *Clin Psychol Rev, 17 (5)*, 451-78.

Kelly, T. M., Cornelius, J. R. & Clark, D. B. (2003). Psychiatric disorders and attempted suicide among adolescents with substance use disorders. *Drug and Alcohol Dependence 73*, 87–97.

Kendler, K. S., Neale, M. C., Maclean, C. J., et al, (1993). Smoking and major depression: a causal analysis. *Arch Gen Psychiatry, 50*, 36-43.

Kenny, P. J., File, S. E. & Rattray, M. (2001). Nicotine regulates 5-HT(1A) receptor gene expression in the cerebral cortex and dorsal hippocampus. *Eur J Neurosci, 13 (6)*, 1267-71.

Kessler, R. C., Berglund, P. A., Borges, G., et al. (2007). Smoking and suicidal behaviors in the National Comorbidity Survey: Replication. *J Nerv Ment Dis, 95*, 369–377.

Kessler, R. C., Borges, G., Sampson, N., et al. (2008). The association between smoking and subsequent suicide-related outcomes in the National Comorbidity Survey panel sample. *Mol Psychiatry* Jul 22

Khaled, S. M., Bulloch, A., Exner, D. V. & Patten, S. B. (2009). Cigarette smoking, stages of change, and major depression in the Canadian population. *Can J Psychiatry, 54 (3)*, 204-8.

King, C. A., Hill, E. M., Naylor, M., et al. (1993). Alcohol consumption in relation to other predictors of suicidality among adolescent

King, R. A., Schwab-Stone, M., Flisher, A. J., et al. (2001). Psychosocial and risk behavior correlates of youth suicide attempts and suicidal ideation. *J Am Acad Child Adolesc Psychiatry 40*, 837-46.

King, R. A., Schwab-Stone, M., Flisher, A. J., et al. (2002). Psychosocial and risk behavior correlates of youth suicide attempts and suicidal ideation. *J Am Acad Child Adolesc Psychiatry 40*, 837–46.

Kirmayer, L. J., Brass, G. M. & Tait, C. L. (2000). The mental health of Aboriginal peoples: Transformations of identity and community. *The Canadian Journal of Psychiatry 45 (7)*, 607–616.

Kotila, L. & Lonnqvist, J. (1988). Adolescent suicide attempts: Sex differences predicting suicide. *Acta Psychiatrica Scandinavica, 77*, 264—270.

Lam, T. H., Stewart, S. M., Yip, P. S., et al, (2004). Suicidality and cultural values among Hong Kong adolescents. *Soc Sci Med., 58*, 487-98.

Larsson, B. & Sund, A. M. (2008). Prevalence, course, incidence and 1-year prediction of deliberate self-harm and suicide attempts in early adolescents. *Suicide Life Threat Behav, 38 (2)*, 152–165.

Lasser, K., Boyd, J. W., Woolhandler, S., et al. (2000). Smoking and mental illness: A population-based prevalence study. *JAMA, 284, (20)*, 2606-10.

Laucht, M., Esser, G. & Schmidt., M. (2000a). Longitudinal research on the developmental epidemiology of mental disorders: Aims, concepts, and major results of the Mannheim Study of At Risk Children. *Zeitschrift fu¨ r Klinische Psychologie. Forschung und Praxis 29*, 246–262.

Laucht, M., Esser, G., Baving, L., et al. (2000b). Behavioral sequlae of perinatal insults and early family adversity at 8 years of age. *Journal of the American Academy of Child and Adolescent Psychiatry, 39*, 1229–1237.

Laucht, M., Schmidt, M. H. & Esser, G. (2002). Motor, cognitive and socio-emotional development of 11-year-olds born with early risks: Late consequences? *Zeitschrift fu¨ r Kinder- und Jugendpsychiatrie, 30*, 5–19

Leistikow, B., (2003). Commentary: Questionable premises, overadjustment, and a smoking/suicide association in younger adult men. *Int J Epidemiol, 32(6),* 1005-6.

Leistikow, B. N. & Shipley, M. J. (1999). Might stopping smoking reduce injury death risks? A meta-analysis of randomized, controlled trials. *Prev Med*, 28, 255–259.

Leistikow, B. N., Martin, D. C. & Samuels, S. J., (2000). Injury death excesses in smokers: a 1990–95 United States national cohort study. *Inj Prev*, *6*, 277–80.

Lerman, C. & Berrettini, W. (2003). Elucidating the role of genetic factors in smoking behavior and nicotine dependence. *Am J Med Gen B Neuropsychiatr Genet, 118b (1),* 48-54.

Lerman, C., Caporaso, N., Main, D., et al. (1998). Depression and self-medication with nicotine: the modifying influence of the dopamine D4 receptor gene. *Health Psychol, 17(1),* 56-62.

Lewinsohn, P. M., Rohde, P. & Seeley, J. R., (1994). Psychosocial risk factors for future adolescent suicide attempts. *J Consult Clin Psychol*, *62 (2)*, 297–305.

Lewinsohn, P. M., Rohde, P., Seeley, J. R. & Baldwin, C. L. (2001). Gender differences in suicide attempts from adolescence to young adulthood. *J Am Acad Child Adolesc Psych*, *40(4)*, 427–434.

Li, M. D. (2003). The genetics of smoking related behavior: a briefreview. *Am J Med Sci*, *326*, 168–173.

Linnoila, V. M. & Virkkunen, M. (1992). Aggression, suicidality, and serotonin. *J Clin Psychiatry*, *53*, 46 –51.

Li-Tzy, W. & Anthony, J. (1999). Tobacco smoking and depressed mood in late childhood and early adolescence. *Am J Public Health*, *89*, 1837–40.

Lohr, J. & Flynn, K. (1992). Smoking and schizophrenia. *Schizophr Res 8*, 93-102.

Makikyro, T. H., Hakko, H. H., Timonen M. J., et al. (2004). Smoking and suicidality among adolescent psychiatric patients. *J Adolesc Health 34*, 250–253.

Malone, K. M., Waternaux, C., Haas, G. L., et al. (2003). Cigarette smoking, suicidal behavior, and serotonin function in major psychiatric disorders. *Am J Psychiatry*, *160*, 773–779.

Mann, J. (1998). The neurobiology of suicide. *Nature Medicine*, *4(1)*, 25–30.

Mann, J. J., Waternaux, C., Haas, G. L., et al. (1999). Toward a clinical model of suicidal behavior in psychiatric patients. *Am J Psychiatry*, *156*, 181–9.

Mann, J. J. (2002). A current perspective of suicide and attempted suicide. *Ann Intern Med*, *136*, 302–11.

Mann, J. J. (2003). Neurobiology of suicidal behaviour. *Nat Rev Neurosci*, *4*, 819–28.

Marcinko, D., Pivac, N., Martinac, M. et al. (2007). Platelet serotonin and serum cholesterol concentrations in suicidal and non-suicidal male patients with a first episode of psychosis. *Psychiatry Res*, *150 (1),* 105-8.

Markou, A., Kosten, T. R. & Koob, G. F. (1998). Neurobiological similarities in depression and drug dependence: a self-medication hypothesis. *Neuropsychopharmacology*, *18*, 135–174.

Martínez-Ortega, J. M., Jurado, D. & Gurpegui, M. (2008). Nicotine dependence vs. daily smoking as a meaningful variable :implications for clinical and epidemiological psychiatric studies. *Prog Neuropsychopharmacol Biol Psychiatry*, *32(8)*, 1972-7.

Marttunen, M. J., Aro, H. M., Henriksson, M. M., et al. (1991). Mental disorders in adolescent suicide. *Arch Gen Psychiatry*, *48*, 834–9.

Maser, J. D., Akiskal, H. S., Schettler, P., et al. (2002). Can temperament identify affectively ill patients who engage in lethal or near-lethal suicidal behavior? A 14-year prospective study. *Suicide Life Threat Behav*, *32*, 10–32.

McAuliffe, C M., (2002). Suicidal ideation as an articulation of intent: a focus for suicide prevention? *Arch Suicide Res*, *6*, 325–338.

McCloud, A., Barnaby, B., Omu, N., et al. (2004). Relationship between alcohol use disorders and suicidality in a psychiatric population. In a patient prevalence study. *Br J Psychiatry*, *184*, 439-445.

McEwen, A., Hajek, P., McRobbie, H. & West, R. (2006). Manual of Smoking Cessation.AGuide for Counsellors and Practitioners. Blackwell Publishing, Oxford, UK.

McGee, R., Feehan, M., Williams, S., et al. (1990). DSM-III disorders in a large sample of adolescents. *J Am Acad Child Adolesc Psychiatry*, *29*, 611–619.

McGee, R., Williams, S. & Nada-Raja, S. (2005). Is cigarette smoking associated with suicidal ideation among young people? *Am J Psychiatry* *162*, 619-20.

McKeown, R. E., Garrison, C. Z., Cuffe, S. P., et al. (1998). Incidence and predictors of suicidal behaviours in a longitudinal sample of adolescents. *J Am Acad Child Adolesc Psychiatry*, *37*, 612-9.

McManus, I. C. & Weeks, S. J. (1982). Smoking, personality and reasons for smoking. *Psychol Med*, *12*, 349-356.

Menti, E., Lekka, N. P., Assimakopoulos, K., et al, (2007). Smoking, psychosocial factors, psychopathologic behavior, and other related conditions in hospitalized youth suicide attempters. *Compr Psychiatry 48 (6)*, 522-8.

Meulemans, W., Van den Broeck, J. & Geldhof, K. (1992). Smoking and suicide. *Lancet*, *340*, 1096.

Miller, M., Hemenway, D. & Rimm, E. (2000). Cigarettes and suicide: a prospective study of 50 000 men. *Am J Public Health*, *90*, 768–73.

Miller, M., Hemenway, D., Bell, N. S. et al. (2000). Cigarette smoking and suicide: a prospective study of 300 000 male active-duty Army soldiers. *Am J Epidemiol*, *151(11)*, 1060–63.

Miller, M., Hemenway, D. & Rimm, E. (2000). Cigarettes and suicide: a prospective study of 50,000 men. *Am J Public Health*, *90(5)*, 768-73.

Miller, T. R. & Taylor, D. M. (2005). Adolescent suicidality: who will ideate, who will act? *Suicide Life Threat Behav*, *35*, 425–435.

Mino, Y., Shigemi, J., Otsu, T., et al. (2000). Does smoking cessation improve mental health? *Psychiatry Clin Neurosci*, *54(2),* 169–72.

Moriya, F. & Hashimoto, Y. (2005). Do Smokers Who Commit Suicide Have High Blood Levels of Nicotine? *Am J Psychiatry*, *162*, 4.

Moriya, F., Hashimoto, Y. & Furumiya, J. (2007). Nicotine and cotinine levels in body fluids of smokers who committed suicide. *Forensic Science International*, *168*, 102–105.

Mück-Seler, D., Jakovljević, M. & Pivac, N. (1996). Platelet 5-HT concentrations and suicidal behaviour in recurrent majordepression. *J Affect Disord*, *39(1),* 73-80.

Murphy, J. M., Horton, N. J., Monson, R. R., et al. (2003). Cigarette smoking in relation to depression: historical trends from the Stirling County Study. *Am J Psychiatry*, *160(9),* 1663-9.

National Center for Health Statistics, (1998). Health, United States, 1998: Socioeconomic status and health chartbook. Hyattsville, MD: Public Health Service

Newcomb, M. D., Huba, G. J. & Bentler, P. M. (1981). A multidimensional assessment of stressful life events among adolescents: Derivation and correlates. *Journal of Health and Social Behavior 22*, 400-415.

Nolen-Hoeksema, S. (1994). An interactive model for the emergence of gender differences in depression in adolescence. *Journal of Research on Adolescence*, *4*, 519-534.

Nrugham, L, Larsson, B & Sund, AM, (2008). Predictors of suicidal acts across adolescence: Influences of familial, peer and individual factors. *J Affec Disorder*, 109, 35–45.

Oquendo, M. A., Galfalvy, H., Russo, S. et al. (2004). Prospective study of clinical predictors of suicidal acts after a major depressive episode in patients with major depressive disorder or bipolar disorder. *Am J Psychiatry 161 (8)*, 1433-41.

Parillo, A. V., Felts, W. M. & Mikow-Porto, V. (1997). Early initiation of sexual intercourse and its co-occurrence with other health risk behaviors in high school students: The 1993 North Carolina youth risk behavior survey. *Journal of Health Education*, 22(2), 85-93.

Parks, H. S., Schepp, K. G., Jang, E. H. & Koo H. Y. (2006). Predictors of suicidal ideation among high school students by gender in South Korea. *J Sch Health, 76*, 181-8.

Patten, C. A., Hurt, R. D., Offord, K. P., et al. (2003). Relationship of tobacco use to depressive disorders and suicidality among patients treated for alcohol dependence. *American Journal on Addictions, 12*, 71–83.

Patton, G., Carlin, J., Coffey, C., et al. (1998). Depression, anxiety, and smoking initiation: a prospective study over 3 years. *Am J Public Health 88,* 1518–21.

Payci, S. O., Ergin, A., Saatci, E., et al. (2005). Suicidal thought and behaviour in high school students in Adana, Turkey. *Coll Antropol*, *29*, 527– 531.

Pedersen, W. & von Soest, T. (2009). Smoking, nicotine dependence and mental health among young adults: a 13-year population-based longitudinal study. *Addiction, 104(1),* 129-37.

Piko, B. F. & Fitzpatrick, K. M. (2004). Substance use, religiosity, and other protective factors among Hungarian adolescents. *Addict Behav*, *29*, 1095–1107.

Pivac, N., Jakovljevic, M., Muck-Seler, D. & Brzovic, Z. (1997). Hypothalamic–pituitary– adrenal axis function and platelet serotonin concentrations in depressed patients. *Psychiatry Res*, *73*, 123–32.

Poirier, M. F., Canceil, O, Baylé, F & et al, (2002). Prevalence of smoking in psychiatric patients. *Prog Neuropsychopharmacol Biol Psychiatry*, *26(3),* 529-37.

Rabenstein, R., Caldarone, B. & Bicciotto, M. (2006). The nicotinic antagonist mecamylamine has antidepressant-like effects in wild-type but not _2- or 7-nicotinic acetylcholine receptor subunit knockout mice. Psychopharmacology, 189, 395–401.

Reynolds, W., (1999). Assessment of suicidal ideation in inner-city children and young adolescents: Reliability and validity of the suicidal ideation questionnaire-JR. *School Psychology Review*, *28*, 17–30.

Riala, K., Taanila, A., Hakko, H. & Räsänen, P. (2009).Longitudinal smoking habits as risk factors for early-onset and repetitive suicide attempts: the Northern Finland 1966 Birth Cohort study. *Ann Epidemiol 19(5),* 329-35.

Riala, K., Viilo, K., Hakko, H. & Rasanen, P. (2007). Heavy daily smoking among under 18-year-old psychiatric inpatients is associated with increased risk for suicide attempts. *European Psychiatry*, *22*, 219-222.

Ribeiro, E. B., Bettiker, R. L., Bogdanov, M. & Wurtman, R. J. (1993). Effects of systemic nicotine on serotonin release in rat brain. *Brain Res*, *621(2),* 311-8.

Rickelman, B. L. & Houfek, J. F. (1995). Toward an interactional model of suicidal behaviors: Cognitive rigidity, attributional style, stress, hopelessness, and depression. *Archives of Psvchiatric Nursing*, *9*, 158-168.

Roggenbach, J., Müller-Oerlinghausen, B., Franke, L., et al. (2007). Peripheral serotonergic markers in acutely suicidal patients. 1. Comparison of serotonergic platelet measures between suicidal individuals, nonsuicidal patients with major depression and healthy subjects. *J Neural Transm*, *114(4),* 479-87.

Rohde, P., Seeley, J. S., Rohling, J. & Rohling, M. (2003). The life attitudes schedule-short form: psychometric properties and correlates of adolescent suicide proneness. *Suicide Life Threat Behav*, *(3)*, 249-260.

Rossow, I, Grohølt, B. & Wichstrøm, L. (2005). Intoxicants and suicidal behaviour among adolescents: changes in levels and associations from 1992 to 2002. *Addiction*, *100(1)*, 79–88.

Royal College of Physicians, (1977). Smoking or Health. London, UK: Pitman Medical.

Rutter, M. (2000). Psychosocial influences: Critiques, findings, and research needs. *Development and Psychopathology*, *12*, 375–405.

Salin-Pascual, R. J., Rosas, M., Jimenez-Genchi, A., et al. (1996). Antidepressant effect of transdermal nicotine patches in non-smoking patients with major depression. *J Clin Psychiatry*, *57*, 387–389.

Schneider, B., Wetterling, T., Georgi, K., et al. (2009). Smoking differently modifies suicide risk of affective disorders, substance use disorders, and social factors. *J Affect Disord*, *112 (1-3),* 165-73.

Schuman, H. & Johnson, M. P. (1976). Attitudes and behaviour. *Annu Rev Sociol*, *2*, 161–207.

Shaffer, D., Gould, M., Fisher, P., et al. (1996). Psychiatric diagnosis in child and adolescent suicide. *Arch Gen Psychiatry*, *53*, 339– 344.

Sher, L. (2006a). Alcohol consumption and suicide. *QJM*, *99(1),* 57-61.

Sher, L, (2006b). Alcohol and suicide: neurobiological and clinical aspects. *Scientific World Journal*, *6,*700-6.

Shneidman, E. S. (1985). Definition of suicide. New York: Wiley

Silagy, C., Lancaster, T., Stead, L., et al. (2004). Nicotine replacement therapy for smoking cessation. *The Cochrane Library, www.thecochranelibrary.com.*

Smith, G. D., Phillips, A. N. & Neaton, J. D. (1992). Smoking as "independent" risk factor for suicide: illustration of an artifact from observational epidemiology? *Lancet*, *340(8821),* 709-12.

Smith, G. M. (1969). Relations between personality and smoking behavior in preadult subjects. *J Consult Clin Psychol*, *33*, 710-715.

Smith, S. & Fiore, M. (1999). The epidemiology of tobacco use, dependence, and cessation in the United States. *Primary Care Clinics in Office Practice*, *26 (3)*, 100-123.

Smith, R C., Singh, A., Infante, M., et al. (2002). Effects of cigarette smoking and nicotine nasal spray on psychiatric symptoms and cognition in schizophrenia. *Neuropsychopharmacology*, *27 (3),* 479–497.

Spijkerman, R., van den Eijnden, R. J., Vitale, S. & Engels, R. C. (2004). Explaining adolescents' smoking and drinking behavior: the concept of smoker and drinker prototypes in relation to variables of the theory of planned behavior. *Addict Behav*, *29*, 1615–1622.

Stålenheim, E. G. (2001). Relationships between attempted suicide, temperamental vulnerability, and violent criminality in a Swedish forensic psychiatric population. *Eur Psychiatry*, *16(7),* 386-94.

Stanley, B., Gameroff, M. J., Michalsen, V., et al. (2001). Are suicide attempters who self-mutilate a unique population? *Am J Psychiatry 158*, 427–32.

Statham, D. J., Heath, A. C., Madden, P. A., et al. (1998). Suicidal behaviour: an epidemiological and genetic study. *Psychol Med*, *28*, 839–855.

Sullivan, P. F., Neale, M. C. & Kendler, K. S. (2000). Genetic epidemiology of major derpression: review and meta-analysis. *Am J Psychiatry*, *157,*1552–1562.

Takakura, M., Ueji, M. & Sakihara, S. (2001). Covariation of cigarette smoking and other health-risk behaviours among Japanese high school students: a preliminary study. *J Epidemiol*, *11*, 224–228.

Tanskanen, A., Tuomiletho, J., Viinamaki, H. et al. (2000). Smoking and the risk of suicide. *Acta Psychiatr Scand*, 101, 243–45.

Tanskanen, A., Viinamaki, H., Hintikka, J., et al. (1998). Smoking and suicidality among psychiatric patients. *Am J Psychiatry*, *155 (1)*, 129-130.

Taylor, J. E., Conard, M. W., Koetting, O., Byrne, K., et al. (2004). Saturation of tobacco smoking models and risk of alcohol and tobacco use among adolescents. *J Adolesc Health,* 35, 190–196.

Tercyak, K. P. & Audrain-McGovern, J. (2003). Personality differences associated with smoking experimentation among adolescents with and without comorbid symptoms of ADHD. *Subst Use Misuse*, *38*, 1953-70.

Terracciano, A. & Costa, Jr P. T. (2004). Smoking and the five-factor model of personality. *Addiction*, *99*, 472-81.

Tomori, M., Zalar, B., Kores Plesnicar, B., et al. (2001). Smoking in relation to psychosocial risk factors in adolescents. *Eur Child Adolesc Psychiatry*, *10*, 143–150.

Toros, F., Bilgin, N. G., Sasmaz, T. et al. (2004). Suicide attempts and risk factors among children and adolescents. *Yonsei Med J*, *45*, 367–374.

Trauth, J. A., Seidler, F. J., Ali, S. F., et al. (2001). Adolescent nicotine exposure produces immediate and long-term changes in CNS noradrenergic and dopaminergic function. *Brain Res*, *892*, 269–80.

Tsoh, J. Y., Humfleet, G. L., Munoz, R. F., et al. (2000). Development of major depression after treatment for smoking cessation. *Am J Psychiatr*, 157, 368–374.

Undheim, A. M. & Sund, A. M. (2005). School factors and the emergence of depressive symptoms among young Norwegian adolescents. *Eur Child Adolesc Psychiatry*, *14*, 446– 453.

Upadhyaya, H. P., Deas, D., Brady, K. T. & Kruesi, M. (2002). Cigarette smoking and psychiatric comorbidity in children and adolescents. *J Am Acad Child Adolesc Psychiatry*, *41*, 1294–1305.

US Department of Health and Human Services, (1990a). Psychological and behavioral consequences and correlates of smoking cessation. In: Health Benefits of Smoking Cessation: A Report of the US Surgeon General. Office on Smoking & Health, Rockville, MD, pp. 517–578.

US Department of Health and Human Services, (1990b). The Health Benefits of Smoking Cessation. A Report of the US Surgeon General. Office on Smoking & Health, Rockville, MD

Verkes, R. J,, Van der Mast, R. C., Kerkhof, A. J., et al. (1998). Platelet serotonin, monoamine oxidase activity, and [3H]paroxetine binding related to impulsive suicide attempts and borderline personality disorder. *Biol Psychiatry, 43(10)*, 740-6.

Vinod, K. Y. & Hungund, B. L. (2006). Role of the endocannabinoid system in depression and suicide. *Trends Pharmacol Sci*, 27, 539–545.

Wadsby, M., Sydsjo, G. & Svedin, C. G. (1998). Evaluation of a short term intervention program for psychosocial-risk mothers and their infants. *Nordic Journal of Psychiatry, 52*, 501–511.

Wadsby, M. Sydsjo, G. & Svedin, C. G. (2001). Evaluation of an intervention programme to support mothers and babies at psychosocial risk: assessment of mother/child interaction and mother's perception of benefit. *Health and Social Care in the Community 9*, 125–133.

Wadsby, M., Svedin, C. G. & Sydsjö, G. (2007). Children of mothers at psychosocial risk growing up: a follow up at the age of 16. *J Adolesc 30 (1)*, 147-64.

Weiser, M., Reichenberg, A., Grotto, I., et al. (2004). Higher rates of cigarette smoking in male adolescents before the onset of schizophrenia: a historical-prospective cohort study. *Am J Psychiatry*, 161, 1219–1223.

Weiss, J. W., Mouttapa, M., Chou, Z. C., et al. (2005). Hostility, depressive symptom, and smoking in early adolescence. *J Adolesc 28*, 49-62.

West, R. & Shiffman, S. (2001). Effect of oral nicotine dosing forms on cigarette withdrawal symptoms and craving: a systematic review. *Psychopharmacology*, 155, 115–122.

Whitfield, J. B., Pang, D., Bucholz, K. K., et al. (2000). Monoamine oxidase: associations with alcohol dependence, smoking and other measures of psychopathology. *Psychol Med, 30(2),* 443-54.

WHO, (2008). Statement World Suicide Prevention Day 10 September.

Wichstrøm, L. & Rossow, I. (2002). Explaining the gender difference in self-reported suicide attempts: A nationally representative study of Norwegian adolescents. *Suicide Life-Threatening Behaviour*, *32(2)*, 101–116.

Wichstrøm, L., (2000). Predictors of adolescent suicide attempts: a nationally representative longitudinal study of Norwegian adolescents. *J Am Acad Child Adolesc Psych 39 (5)*, 603–610.

Wilson, K. G., Stelzer, J., Bergman, JN & et al, (1995). Problem solving, stress, and coping in adolescent suicide attempts. *Suicide and Life Threatening Behavior*, *25*, 241-252.

Windle, M., (1992). A longitudinal study of stress buffering for adolescent problem behaviors. *Developmental Psychology, 28*, 522-530.

Windle, RC & Windle, M, (1997). An investigation of adolescents' substance use behaviors, depressed affect, and suicidal behaviors. *J Child Psychol Psychiatry*, *38*, 921-9.

Woods, E. R., Lin, Y., Middleman, A., et al. (1997). The associations of suicide attempts in adolescents. *Pediatric*, *99*, 791–796.

Wu, P., Hoven, C. W., Liu, X., et al. (2004). Substance use, suicidal ideation and attempts in children and adolescents. *Suicide Life Threat Behav*, *34*, 408–420.

Xu, J., Mendrek, A., Cohen, M. S., et al. (2007). Effect of cigarette smoking on prefrontal cortical function in nondeprived smokers performing the Stroop Task. *Neuropsychopharmacology*, *32(6),* 1421-8.

Xu, Z., Seidler, F., Cousins, M., et al. (2002). Adolescent nicotine administration alters serotonin receptors and cell signaling mediated through adenyl cyclase. *Brain Res*, *951*, 280 –292.

Yang, Y. K., Nelson, L., Kamaraju, L., et al. (2002). Nicotine decreases bradykinesia-rigidity in haloperidol-treated patients with schizophrenia. *Neuropsychopharmacology*, *27(4),* 684–686.

INDEX

B

C

D

E

F

G

H

I

N

O

P

Q

R

S